Quechua-Spanish Bilingualism

Language Acquisition & Language Disorders

Volumes in this series provide a forum for research contributing to theories of language acquistion (first and second, child and adult), language learnability, language attrition and language disorders.

Series Editors

Harald Clahsen
University of Essex

Lydia White
McGill University

Editorial Board

Melissa F. Bowerman
Max Planck Institut für Psycholinguistik, Nijmegen

Katherine Demuth
Brown University

Wolfgang U. Dressler
Universität Wien

Nina Hyams
University of California at Los Angeles

Jürgen M. Meisel
Universität Hamburg

William O'Grady
University of Hawaii

Mabel Rice
University of Kansas

Luigi Rizzi
University of Siena

Bonnie D. Schwartz
University of Hawaii at Manao

Antonella Sorace
University of Edinburgh

Karin Stromswold
Rutgers University

Jürgen Weissenborn
Universität Potsdam

Frank Wijnen
Utrecht University

Volume 35

Quechua-Spanish Bilingualism: Interference and convergence in functional categories
by Liliana Sánchez

Quechua-Spanish Bilingualism
Interference and convergence
in functional categories

Liliana Sánchez

Rutgers University

John Benjamins Publishing Company

Amsterdam / Philadelphia

The paper used in this publication meets the minimum requirements of American National Standard for Information Sciences – Permanence of Paper for Printed Library Materials, ANSI Z39.48-1984.

Library of Congress Cataloging-in-Publication Data

Sánchez, Liliana
    Quechua-Spanish bilingualism : interference and convergence in
        functional categories / Liliana Sánchez.
    p. cm. (Language Acquisition & Language Disorders, ISSN 0925–0123 ; v. 35)
    Includes bibliographical references and indexes.
    1. Bilingualism in children--Peru. 2. Languages in contact--Peru. 3. Quechua language--Grammar, Comparative--Spanish. 4. Spanish Language--Grammar, Comparative--Quechua. 5. Interference (Linguistics). 6. Language acquisition.

    P115 .2 2003
                                                                    2003063845
    ISBN 90 272 5294 7 (Eur.) / 1 58811 471 6 (US) (Hb; alk. paper)

© 2003 – John Benjamins B.V.
No part of this book may be reproduced in any form, by print, photoprint, microfilm, or any other means, without written permission from the publisher.

John Benjamins Publishing Co. · P.O. Box 36224 · 1020 ME Amsterdam · The Netherlands
John Benjamins North America · P.O. Box 27519 · Philadelphia PA 19118-0519 · USA

Table of contents

Acknowledgements   XI

CHAPTER 1
The acquisition of functional categories in bilinguals   1
1.1   Universal Grammar and bilingual language acquisition   2
1.2   The goals of this study   5
1.3   L1, L2 and bilingual acquisition of functional categories   7
1.4   The role of code-mixing in the bilingual steady state   11
1.5   Functional interference and functional convergence in bilingual syntax   12

CHAPTER 2
The direct object system of Quechua and Spanish   17
2.1   Functional features in the direct object system   17
2.2   The direct object system of Quechua: Word order and pronominalization   29
    2.2.1   Canonical word order in Quechua   29
    2.2.2   Fronted direct objects   31
    2.2.3   Fronted verbs   34
    2.2.4   Null D and strong pronouns   37
2.3   The direct object system in Spanish: Word order and clitic-related constructions   40
    2.3.1   Canonical word order in Spanish   40
    2.3.2   Fronted direct objects and clitic-left dislocated structures   43
    2.3.3   Fronted verbs   46
    2.3.4   Clitic and clitic doubling structures as related to Topic or Focus   47
    2.3.5   Null objects   50
    2.3.6   Contrasting the two direct object systems   52

2.4 Studies on direct objects, pronominal systems and word order in L1, L2 and bilingual situations involving Quechua and/or Spanish   53
    2.4.1 Direct objects in first language acquisition   54
        2.4.1.1 Direct objects in Quechua first language acquisition   54
        2.4.1.2 Direct objects in Spanish first language acquisition   56
    2.4.2 Direct objects in second language acquisition   59
        2.4.2.1 Direct objects in Spanish as a second language   59
    2.4.3 Direct objects in bilingual language acquisition   63

Chapter 3
Bilinguals in a language contact situation   65
3.1 The language contact and language shift situations   65
3.2 The geographical areas of language contact   68
    3.2.1 Bilingualism in the district of Ulcumayo   68
    3.2.2 Bilingualism in the district of Wayku, Lamas   70
    3.2.3 "Monolingual" San Juan de Miraflores   72
    3.2.4 Bilingual and "monolingual" participants   73
3.3 Patterns of linguistic input at home   75
3.4 Patterns of linguistic input at school   79
3.5 Measuring linguistic knowledge of bilinguals in a language shift situation   81
    3.5.1 Picture-based story-telling task   82
    3.5.2 Picture–sentence matching task   82
    3.5.3 Conditions for data elicitation   83

Chapter 4
***A turtle is looking at a toad*: Functional interference and convergence in bilingual Quechua**   85
4.1 Story-telling task results in bilingual Quechua   85
    4.1.1 Consistency in the type of verbs used in the narratives   86
    4.1.2 Distribution of direct objects in bilingual Quechua   91
    4.1.3 Evidence for functional convergence: The dropping of accusative marking, the emergence of overt D, and SVO word order   96
        4.1.3.1 Emergence of an indefinite determiner   99
        4.1.3.2 Distribution of (S)OV/VO structures   101
    4.1.4 Distribution of direct objects and their antecedents in discourse   106

4.1.5 Distribution of direct object complements according to their antecedents   110

CHAPTER 5
The frog is looking at Phi-features: Functional convergence in bilingual Spanish   115
5.1 Story-telling task results in bilingual Spanish   116
    5.1.1 Consistency in the type of verbs used by the children in the narratives   117
    5.1.2 Distribution of direct object complements in Spanish narratives: Clitic and D features as evidence of interference and convergence   118
    5.1.3 Distribution of direct object antecedents   129
    5.1.4 Distribution of direct object complements according to their antecedent   131
5.2 Picture–sentence matching task results in bilingual Spanish   146

CHAPTER 6
Conclusions   155
6.1 Summary of main results   155
    6.1.1 Differences and similarities between bilingual acquisition at the steady state and L1 acquisition   157
    6.1.2 Similarities between bilingual and L2 acquisition   156
6.2 Implications for bilingual acquisition theories   157
6.3 Future research   158

Appendix   159

Bibliography   177

Index   185

Acknowledgements

This book was possible thanks to the collaboration of many people. I would like to thank them all. Thanks to Carnegie Mellon University and to the Center for Latin American Studies at the University of Pittsburgh for supporting field research in Peru. Thanks to my colleagues at Carnegie Mellon for their support and camaraderie and to Rutgers University for financial support for editing, data processing and electronic data storage. I would also like to thank my colleagues at Rutgers for their support during the writing process.

Thanks to the people of Ulcumayo and the people of Lamas for welcoming me. Anchata agradisyki wayqipanaykuna. Very special thanks to Mercedes Orosco for introducing me to her hometown and to her wonderful family. Without her support in Ulcumayo, Lima and Highland Park, this project could have never been completed. Thanks also to the administrators and teachers at the Escuela Mariategui, Escuela Tupac Amaru and the community of Apan, especially to Simeon Quiquia for his support. Thanks to all the children who participated in this study in Ulcumayo because they allowed us to have a window into their minds and their hearts. Thanks also because you still speak Quechua no matter what. In Lamas, very special thanks to Jaime Doherty who introduced me to the wonderful town of Wayku and whose contagious love for Lamas Kechwa and for the Lamista people was very inspiring to me. Thanks also to Toribio Amasifuen, Jose Sangama, Misael Sangama, Inocente Sangama, Marcos Tuanama for their collaboration in this project and to all the children who participated in the study. Thank you all for allowing us to share your experiences and your hopes on Bilingual Education. ¡Kausachun Kechwa! I would also like to thank the school administrators, teachers and students of Colegio Pachacutec in San Juan de Miraflores.

Thanks to the research assistants who participated in the fieldwork in Ulcumayo and Lamas in the pilot study and in the main study data collection: (in alphabetical order): Omar Beas, Jose Camacho, Vidal Carvajal, Lidia Chang, Milagros Lucero, Katia Murillo, Jaime Navarrete, José Riqueros and Irma Sanchez.

Thanks also to those who joined us for the transcribing and coding stages of the project: Beto Eliás and Lourdes Tenguan.

I am indebted to Pieter Muysken for his comments on an earlier manuscript and for his comments as a reviewer. Thanks also to Mark Baker, María Blume, Rodolfo Cerrón-Palomino, Silvina Montrul and Jacqueline Toribio for their comments and suggestions and encouragement and to reviewer Joyce Bruhn de Garavito for carefully reading the manuscript and for her very valuable suggestions. I would also like to thank to the audiences at the 3rd International Symposium on Bilingualism and the 4th Conference on the Acquisition of Spanish and Portuguese. Thanks to Tamara Al-Kasey for her proof-editing work and her suggestions and to Phillip Rothwell and Tom Stephens.

And for your love, patience, support and understanding, thanks José, Yesica and Lucía. As always, all errors in this book are mine.

> *To my families: José, Yesi and Lucía*
> *and Irma, Irmita y Cucha.*
>
> *This book is about both sides of the story.*
>
> *Paykuna nipaakushuptiqa, yarpapaakinki chay kwintuta.*

CHAPTER 1

The acquisition of functional categories in bilinguals

The representation of two linguistic systems in the bilingual mind has been the subject of research since the early decades of the past century. It has evolved from the seminal research on the representation of the lexicon in the bilingual mind through diary studies (Ronjat 1913, Leopold 1939, 1949) to linguistic approaches such as the structuralist work on language contact by Weinrich (1968), studies on pathology and lateralization among bilinguals (Paradis 1985, 1990), case studies on bilingual language development (De Houwer 1990, Taeschner 1983, and Lanza 1997, Deuchar and Quay 2000 among others) and research focusing on the interaction between Universal Grammar (UG) (Chomsky 1986a) and linguistic input in two languages (Meisel 1986, 1989, Paradis and Genesse 1996, Nicoladis and Genesee 1997 among others).

This book explores the long-term effects of the interaction between UG and input in two languages on the syntactic representation of bilinguals who live in language contact and language shift situations and who activate their two languages constantly. It focuses on the issue of interference and convergence in the functional features associated with the direct object system among Quechua-Spanish bilinguals assuming a minimalist approach to syntactic representation. Two main hypotheses guide this book: the Functional Interference Hypothesis and the Functional Convergence Hypothesis. The first one aims to account for the role that interference in functional features has in generating syntactic changes in the languages spoken by the bilingual individual and the second one tries to delineate the conditions under which a fusion of functional features takes place in the bilingual mind. The findings of a study that examined the oral production of two groups of Quechua-Spanish bilingual children (8–13) living in a language contact situation as well as the oral production of a comparison group of Spanish-speaking children provide evidence in favor of these two hypotheses. The book is organized as follows. The first chapter presents the background which contextualizes the debate on interaction between UG and input in first, second language and bilingual acquisition and presents the two hypotheses that guide the study. The second chapter focuses on the syntactic representations proposed for the direct object systems in Quechua and Spanish and presents the findings of previous studies on the L1 and L2 acquisition of direct objects. The third chapter presents the participants' bilingual environment and the data collection and coding methodologies employed in the study. The fourth and fifth chapters discuss the Quechua and the Spanish data, respectively, and analyze the evidence in favor of syntactic changes triggered by functional interference and convergence.

1.1   Universal Grammar and bilingual language acquisition

In Universal Grammar (UG) models of language acquisition, research has focused on the interaction between innate principles and linguistic input in the language acquirer's mind. Research on the acquisition of syntax has been characterized by the identification of the initial or default settings for universal principles and the language-specific values assigned to them. As stated by Chomsky, UG is "a theory of the initial state of the language faculty prior to any linguistic experience." (Chomsky 1986a, p. 3, 4)[1] In normal development, this initial state evolves and goes through different stages in the child's mind, "reaching a relatively steady state that undergoes little subsequent change apart from the lexicon." (Chomsky 1995 p. 14) This steady state is the attained grammar.

In the case of bilinguals, interaction between UG and linguistic input is more complex because there are several possibilities that affect this interaction in the course of language development. Assuming the child has had constant exposure to input in the two languages, there are at least three possible scenarios:

1. The child does not differentiate between the two sources of input and treats them initially as a unified system but later on differentiates between two systems (Volterra and Taeschner 1978).
2. The child differentiates the two sources of linguistic input and develops two independent systems, that is, at the steady state the child has two attained grammars (Meisel 1986, 1989, Genesee 1989, Paradis and Genesee 1996).
3. The child differentiates the two sources of linguistic input and develops two independent systems. However, during acquisition there are certain areas of cross-linguistic interference between the two grammars. The degree of

---

1. See also Chomsky (1993).

cross-linguistic influence is variable depending on linguistic factors such as input in one language that reinforces a particular non target-like analysis of the other language (Müller and Hulk 2001), and extra-linguistic variables such as frequency of exposure to the languages and psychological and social factors.

In the field of bilingual syntax acquisition, research has centered on the debate on interdependence versus autonomy of the two syntactic systems. Based on evidence from Italian-German bilingual children, Volterra and Taeschner (1978) proposed that it is possible for a child to develop a single syntactic system for two languages and keep the two lexicons apart.[2] This view as well as the analysis of some extreme cases of code-mixing[3] as in the case of Media Lengua, a language characterized by Quechua morphology and syntax and Spanish lexicon (Muysken 2000) correspond to this scenario.

On the other hand, Paradis and Genesee (1996) define interdependence as the "systemic influence of one language on the grammar of another language during language acquisition" p. 3. This influence causes differences between bilingual and monolingual patterns of language acquisition and rates of language development. Studies such as De Houwer (1990), Paradis and Genesee (1996) and Meisel (1986, 1989), among others, have shown evidence of autonomous syntactic development in early childhood bilingualism. Their findings suggest that two syntactic systems can remain separate in the bilingual mind during the course of acquisition and therefore support the second scenario that we described earlier.

However, there is evidence of transfer in bilingual child language acquisition research (Müller 1998) and cross-linguistic influence (Müller and Hulk 2001). Müller and Hulk (2001) argue in favor of mapping-induced influence. In their view, this type of cross-linguistic influence "occurs only in those domains of the grammar where the learner is confronted with positive evidence

---

2. Romaine (1995) notes that Meisel (1989) has challenged this proposal based on the fact that it involved an Italian-dominant bilingual child.

3. The phenomenon of code-mixing is a very complex one that involves a wide range of mixing possibilities and an enormous amount of variation in linguistic and extra-linguistic factors. UG-based theories on code-mixing propose that it is limited by formal constraints such as Government (Di Sciullo, Muysken and Singh 1986) or constraints that apply to functional categories in the two languages such as the Functional Head Constraint (Belazi, Rubio and Toribio 1994, Toribio 2001). Code-mixing is not the central topic of this study, but in Section 1.4 of this chapter, a brief discussion of the long term effects of language contact and code-mixing on bilingual syntax will be presented.

for more than one possible structural analysis in one language and the other language favors/reinforces one of the two (or more) analysis" (p. 17). This view corresponds to the third scenario, in particular in those cases in which extra-linguistic factors do not have an important influence on cross-linguistic interference.

The debate on bilingual language acquisition under the UG-theoretical perspective has centered on the mechanisms through which the child initially posits one or two differentiated grammars. The studies cited as part of this debate have focused on the early stages of acquisition of the two grammars. There are, however, cases in which cross-linguistic interference remains to be the case once the steady state of the two grammars has been attained. Additional evidence of interdependent systems among bilingual adults comes from contact-induced language change studies (Thomason and Kaufman 1988). In language contact situations, in which societal bilingualism is the case, the two languages spoken by the bilingual undergo significant changes as evidenced in the speech of bilinguals (Appel and Muysken 1987, Romaine 1995, Thomason and Kaufman 1988 among others). Thomason and Kaufman (1988) have proposed that such changes, which they term "linguistic interference", are related to the social status of the two languages involved. They distinguish between contact-induced changes in language maintenance and in language shift situations. In each type of situation, multiple social variables such as the relative size of the minority language community of speakers with respect to the dominant language community as well as the intensity and frequency of contact defined in terms of time and level of bilingualism are crucial predictors of language interference. They dispute the notion that structural linguistic similarities or dissimilarities can serve as appropriate predictors of contact-induced language change. In their view, a particular array of socio-linguistic factors is a better predictor of change than linguistic structure. This view allows for variation in the steady grammars attained by bilinguals, which depends on extra-linguistic factors.

Thus, the evidence is mixed: some research on early childhood bilingual acquisition has shown that the development of autonomous syntactic representations concerning functional categories is possible. Research on the acquisition of functional categories that focuses on the relationship between pragmatics and syntax, and studies on contact-induced language change and code-mixing have both shown that interference between the syntactic systems of the bilingual does take place. In some extreme cases, researchers have posited a single syntactic system processing two lexicons in the bilingual mind, at least in the initial stages.

1.2 The goals of this study

The evidence in favor of autonomous development is very strong and I do not intend to challenge it. At the same time, there appears to be evidence of cross-linguistic interference at the "steady" state among bilinguals living in language contact situations. I will assume the position that, even if extra-linguistic factors are at the basis of this phenomenon, there must be a linguistic representation for it. Thus, the two questions that I will address in this book are:

i. How is cross-linguistic influence at the steady state represented in the bilingual mind?
ii. What are the linguistic mechanisms that allow for interference in some areas of the grammar?

In order to answer these questions, I investigate the evidence of cross-linguistic interference in the attained grammars of two groups of Quechua-Spanish bilingual children (8–13) who live in language contact situations. I focus on the syntactic representations of the direct object systems in their two languages for reasons that will be explained in detail in Chapter 2. The subjects are second-generation bilinguals living in bilingual communities in Peru characterized by language shift from Quechua into Spanish.[4] The main goal of this study is to provide a formal account of the linguistic mechanisms that operate in cases of syntactic cross-linguistic influence.

I will contrast the data obtained from these two groups with data from a Spanish-speaking group of children who live in a Spanish-dominant community who have at least one parent or caretaker who is a Quechua-Spanish bilingual.[5] The goal of this comparison is to show differences in the steady state that are due to variations in the frequency of linguistic input along a language contact continuum.

I selected these two groups because their speech shows evidence of cross-linguistic influence in the two languages. Both Quechua and Spanish are null

---

4. See Chapter 3 for a complete description of the subjects.
5. Unfortunately, there is no monolingual community of Quechua-speaking children for these two varieties and therefore it is not possible to compare their actual syntactic representations. The two varieties of Quechua involved are Lamas Quechua and Northern-Junin Quechua, both have been described in traditional grammars (Coombs, Coombs and Weber 1976 and Black, Bolli and Ticsi 1990) but, to the best of my knowledge, there are no studies on first language acquisition in those varieties.

subject languages with rich subject agreement systems on the verb. They differ in their canonical word order; Quechua is an SOV language while Spanish has an SVO canonical word order. They also differ with respect to the availability of null objects; in Spanish null objects are indefinite or generic but in Quechua they may be definite. Spanish has overt direct object clitics for all persons, whereas third person agreement morphemes for direct objects are null in Quechua (see Chapter 2 for a detailed discussion of the grammar of the two languages).

The evidence of cross-linguistic influence from Spanish on Quechua comes from the dropping of the traditional accusative marker *-ta* and the emergence of indefinite determiners. The first type of interference is exemplified in sentence (1) where the otherwise obligatory *-ta* suffix is absent on the direct object *chay sapito* "that little toad":

Lamas Quechua (Participant L14)
(1) Chay niñito apunta-yka-n chay sapito.
 that boy points-DUR-3SG that little toad
 'That boy points at that little toad.'

The second type is exemplified in sentence (2) which has two indefinite articles where monolingual varieties of Quechua would have null articles:

Lamas Quechua (Participant L2)
(2) Suk wambriyu api-yka-n   suk papel-ta.
 a   boy   grab-DUR-3SG a   paper-ACC
 'A boy grabs a piece of paper.'

There is also evidence of interference in a higher frequency of post-verbal objects in Bilingual Quechua. In sentence (3) the object *achkita* 'doggy' is not focalized and thus should appear in pre-verbal position. In fact, it appears in post-verbal position:

Lamas Quechua
(3) Abrasa-yka-n achk-ita-n-ta.
 hug-DUR-3SG dog-DIM-3SG-ACC
 '(He) is hugging his dog.'

Evidence of Quechua's influence on Spanish comes from null object pronouns with definite antecedents and from gender and number mismatches between clitic pronouns and their antecedents.

Sentences (4) and (5) illustrate the presence of a null object pronoun with a definite and specific antecedent, a characteristic of Quechua grammar and contact varieties of Spanish that is not shared by monolingual varieties of Spanish:[6]

Lamas Bilingual Spanish (Participant L28)
(4) ⟨chay[7]⟩ [//] **ese wamrillu**$_i$ (e)stá metiendo su mano en el cartón
⟨*that*⟩ [//] that boy   is   putting his hand in the board
'That boy is putting his hand inside the cardboard'
y   tortuga (e)stá mirando **pro**$_i$.
and turtle   is   looking pro
'And the turtle is looking at him.'

Sentence (6) shows the use of a feminine clitic with a masculine antecedent that was previously mentioned in sentence (5):

(5) **el otro sapo**$_i$.
the other toad$_i$
'the other toad'
...

(6) y   el perro **la**$_i$ quiere comer.
and the dog CL-FEM$_i$ wants to eat
'And the dog wants to eat her.'

Finally, there is also evidence from word order. In (7) the object DP *su pierna* 'his leg' appears in pre-verbal position, contrary to the canonical post-verbal position it has in Standard Spanish. The object is not focalized.

Bilingual Spanish
(7) Su pierna está poniendo por arriba.
his leg   is   putting up
'(He) is putting his leg up'

In order to analyze this evidence, it is necessary to present an overview of the theoretical framework in which functional categories have been studied in first language (L1), second language (L2) and bilingual acquisition.

---

6. See Escobar (1978), Escobar (1990), Camacho, Paredes and Sanchez (1997), Sanchez (1998), among others for references to this grammatical characteristic of Spanish varieties in contact with Quechua.

7. The child uses the word *chay* 'this' in Quechua.

1.3 L1, L2 and bilingual acquisition of functional categories

In the minimalist framework (Chomsky 1995), the innate language acquisition device is composed of a computational system of human language and the lexicon. The computational system consists of a limited number of operations that generate an infinite number of sound-meaning pairings that are linguistic expressions. The lexicon, on the other hand, is divided into two types of categories: lexical and functional. Cross-linguistic variation resides in variations in the feature specification of functional categories (Ouhalla 1991). Functional categories are the central objects of study in UG-based theories of language acquisition because complete acquisition of their feature specifications constitutes the attained grammar.

The role of functional categories has been the center of the recent debate on first, second language and bilingual acquisition theories based on Universal Grammar syntactic models. The debate is relevant to this study because it has explored the issue of the specification of functional categories from the initial stage through subsequent stages until the steady state is attained. Evidence of cross-linguistic interference among bilinguals indicates that the complete separation of two sets of parametric values for functional categories is not always achieved. In first language acquisition in monolingual communities, functional categories are fully specified at the earliest stages of acquisition; or, if one assumes that they are specified later, they follow relatively straightforward developmental patterns. In second language and bilingual acquisition, attainment of a complete specification for functional categories involves higher levels of complexity. In this study, I will propose a syntactic mechanism that accounts for convergence in the feature specification of functional categories among bilinguals living in a language contact situation. Before presenting the specific proposal to be developed in this book, I will present the debate on the theoretical status of functional categories in first, second and bilingual acquisition.

In first language acquisition, the debate on functional categories has centered on the three logical possibilities for their specification:

A. The strong continuity approach. Early grammar is like adult grammar. All functional projections are present at the initial stage of language development. There might be differences in the use of some syntactic structures but these can be attributed to the lack of knowledge of selectional or pragmatic restrictions (Hyams 1994, 1996, Rizzi 1993/1994, Deprez and Pierce 1993, 1994) or to a default setting (Platzack 1996).

B. The maturational approach. The initial state or early grammar includes only lexical categories. More specifically, in this view early grammar is conceived as a lexical-thematic system in which thematic structures are mapped onto lexical-syntactic structures (Borer and Wexler 1987, Radford 1990). Under this view, functional projections are not present at the initial stages of language acquisition.

C. The weak continuity approach. The principles of X'-Theory are available to the child from the initial stage but phrase structure positions emerge gradually (Pinker 1984, Lebeaux 2000). In particular, Clahsen, Eissenbesiss and Vainikka (1994) have proposed that functional categories such as D are not present at the initial stages but are developed in later stages.

This debate has been echoed in the field of second language acquisition as a debate on the initial syntactic representation of second language learners. The issue of whether functional categories are A) fully specified at the initial L2 stage of language development as in the L1, B) are absent from such representations, or C) are present but underspecified has been explored in work by Schwartz and Sprouse (1996), Epstein, Flynn and Martohardjiono (1996), Vainikka and Young-Scholten (1996), and Eubank (1993/4), respectively.[8] More recently, Van de Craats, Corver and Van Hout (2000) have presented a minimalist perspective on the issue of second language and bilingual syntactic representations. Following the current minimalist viewpoint, they assume a single computational system operating in the mind of the second language acquirer and the bilingual. This system serves as the basis of language development in the two languages. Given this unique Computational System, cross-linguistic syntactic differences arise as a result of a differentiation in the lexicon of the two languages. Thus, they focus on the process by which a monolingual reaches a bilingual target state by developing two distinct lexicons (L1 lexicon versus L2 lexicon). The two lexicons in the bilingual mind vary along different parametric values. These involve:

> "i. A choice of categories from the UG-defined inventory of lexical and functional categories;
> ii. An ordering relation between a categorial head x^0 and its complement (the head parameter)

---

8. Herschensohn (2000) proposes that L2 grammars are constrained by UG, that is, interlanguages are not wild grammars. However, they differ from L1 grammars because L2 learners resort to a coalition of supplementary learning strategies as well as to instruction and feedback in addition to processing of the linguistic input.

iii. A strength feature determining the overtness or covertness of displacement" p. 225.

Their definition of lexicon, however, includes along with the knowledge of arbitrary sound-meaning pairings, knowledge of the set of formal features (FFs) contained in the coding of a lexical item. In their model, the initial state of L2 acquisition is characterized by L1 vocabulary and L1 parameter settings. Interlanguage states are characterized by L2 vocabulary and L1 syntax. This characterization aims to show the "linguistic conservatism" of the L1 parametric values by the L2 acquirer. At the bilingual target, the bilingual mind has a fully developed L2 vocabulary and L2 parameter values. Thus, their view is one in which there is a gradual replacement of the L1 specification of the FFs of functional categories by the L2 specifications under the assumption of an initial state of Full Transfer.

In studies on bilingual early language acquisition, the debate has centered on the issue of independent or cross-linguistic influence on the functional categories of the languages acquired by the child. Paradis and Genesee (1996) have shown that the specifications for functional categories are distinct and autonomous in the mind of the bilingual child. On the other hand, Müller (1998) has shown that even in cases in which bilingual children are equally dominant in both languages, transfer of grammatical properties from one language into the other does take place. She argues that this is the case when one of the languages contains ambiguous input compatible with more than one analysis of a particular aspect of its grammar. If input in the other language is unambiguous, then transfer acts as a relief strategy for the child. Müller proposes that the features transferred are those of specific functional categories. In this book, I will pursue this line of analysis, under the assumption that in the particular language contact situations that I will analyze, input has a high degree of variation and is compatible with multiple analyses for functional features associated with categories such as determiners and clitics. However, I will focus not on the transfer that takes place at the early stages of acquisition but on inter-linguistic transfer in functional features that becomes part of the two attained grammars. I will also argue that there is a subset of cases of cross-linguistic interference that result in convergence in the feature specification of the same functional categories in the two languages.

1.4 The role of code-mixing in the bilingual steady state

One additional factor to consider in the attainment of two grammars by bilingual children in a language contact situation is the role that the constant practice of borrowing and code-mixing plays in bilingual acquisition (Poplack, Sankoff and Miller 1988, Musyken 2000, Jake, Myers-Scotton and Gross 2002 among others). Di Sciullo, Muysken and Singh (1986), Belazi, Rubin and Toribio (1994) and Toribio (2001) have shown a complex picture in which formal constraints such as the Government Constraint or the Functional Head Constraint operate in the bilingual but in which the feature specification of the functional categories among bilinguals does not necessarily remain unaffected by bilingualism. In the data I analyze in the present study, cross-linguistic influence appears also as cases of code-mixing. The following sentence from one of the bilingual children in this study illustrates a structure in which one of the nominal lexical bases is a Spanish insertion. In addition, the verb has a Spanish origin:[9]

Bilingual Lamas Quechua
(8) Suk wambriyo *abrasa*-yka-n   suk *sap-ito*.
     a   boy   hug-PROG-3SG one toad-DIM
     'A boy is hugging a little toad.'

I will follow Muysken's (2000) proposal that these are cases of lexical insertion. Muysken distinguishes between insertion at the x^0-level and insertion at the XP-level. In a language such as Quechua the type of insertion at the x^0-level can be thought of as the insertion of a lexical category or insertion of a functional category. Indeed, Muysken (2000) has described a variety of Quechua, Media Lengua, that is characterized by the use of a Spanish lexicon with Quechua grammatical morphemes:

(9) *Chicha*-da *xora*-mi   *irbi*-chi-*ndu*   *ahi*-munda-mi
     Chicha-ACC corn-FOC   boil-CAUS-SUB   there-ABL-FOC
     sirni-nchi *ahi*-munda-ga *dulsi*-da   *poni*-nchi.
     strain-1PL there-ABL-TOP sweet-ACC   put-1PL
     'As to chicha, having boiled corn first, we strain (it) and then we put (it) in sugar' (Muysken 2000, p. 19).

---

9. See Dominguez (2000) for an experimental study on Quechua-Spanish code-switching.

Muysken notes that "all the lexical bases in Media Lengua are Spanish, the affixes all Quechua (with the exception of the gerundive marker -ndu < Sp ndo) and the general word order and syntax Quechua." (Muysken 2000, p. 19)

The two varieties of Bilingual Quechua studied in this book show instances of lexical insertion that contrast with the monolingual varieties described in traditional grammars. Examples (10) in bilingual Quechua and (11) in monolingual Quechua illustrate this contrast. The Spanish lexical items inserted are in italics:

Bilingual Ulcumayo Quechua
(10) *Chibolu*-taq *sapu*-ta *agarra*-ya-n
boy-CONTR toad-ACC grab-PROG-3SG
'The boy grabbed the toad'

Monolingual Ulcumayo Quechua
(11) Wamra-taq agash-ta chala-ya-n
boy-CONTR frog-ACC grab-PROG-3SG
'The boy grabbed the frog'

In (10), there is lexical insertion of Spanish bases but the word order remains canonical SOV as in monolingual Quechua and the direct object is marked for accusative case. Example (8) from the bilingual Lamas Quechua data contrasts with the example (12) below. The sentence in (8) has SVO word order and there is dropping of the accusative marking from the direct object.

Monolingual Lamas Quechua
(12) Suk wamra suk kurtashu-ta uklla-yka-n
a boy a frog-ACC hug-PROG-3SG
'A boy is hugging a frog'

Examples (8) and (12) are an indication that there may be long-term effects of insertion on the bilingual grammar. I will propose, however, that lexical insertion does not necessarily lead to syntactic changes in the two languages in contact, but that cross-linguistic interference in functional features may lead to syntactic changes due to convergence of the features at the steady state.

1.5 Functional interference and functional convergence in bilingual syntax

Previous definitions of interference and convergence have emerged from the analysis of language contact situations. The terms have been used previously in the literature about contact-induced language change to refer to the transfer of syntactic properties from one language into another that results in structural similarities between the two languages (Rozencvejg 1976).[10] As I take the position that language contact takes place in the mind of bilinguals, my definition of interference and convergence refers to two systems of functional features competing in the bilingual mind.

I assume a view of functional features as minimal units that cannot be derived from other properties of the grammar. I also assume that they are distinct from lexical entries. Furthermore, I assume that there is parametric variation with respect to the set of functional features associated with a functional projection. Thus, gender features might be associated with the functional projection D in language A, but not in Language B. In cases of bilingualism in which the set of features associated with a category in language A differs from those associated with an equivalent category in language B, the matrix of features may contain different combinations of features from languages A and B. Bilinguals can develop two distinct sets of features for equivalent categories in the two languages and these are cases such as those analyzed by Paradis and Genesse (1996), but there might be interference in the feature specifications of the two languages in such a way that certain features not activated in one of the languages become activated by input in the other as proposed by Müller and Hulk (2001). I would like to propose that interference in functional features in the grammar of bilinguals triggers syntactic changes. This is formalized in the:

Functional Interference Hypothesis
Functional interference in bilinguals, i.e. the activation of functional features in one language triggered by input in the other language, generates syntactic changes in the bilingual grammars. Interference in lexical entries (n-insertion, v-insertion) does not generate such changes.

This hypothesis predicts that it should be possible to relexify a language by insertion of lexical categories at the x^0-level without altering the syntax of a language. Muysken's (2000) analysis of Media Lengua data shows precisely such a case. It also predicts that changes in the syntax occur only when there is interference in the specification of functional features. That is, it should be

---

10. More specifically, Rozencvejg (1976) dubs this type of convergence "indirect convergence." He defines it as "the replacement in one and/or both languages of the characteristics and rules peculiar to it with corresponding (synonymous) characteristics and rules shared by both contact languages" p. 33.

possible to encounter language contact situations in which, despite a low frequency of insertion of lexical categories, changes in the syntax take place due to interference in functional features.

In this book, I will present evidence from a language contact situation in which interference in functional features of categories such as determiners and clitics has resulted in changes in the syntax of the two languages spoken by Quechua-Spanish bilinguals affecting word order and the distribution of null objects. Such interference has taken place in spite of relatively low levels of lexical borrowing of nouns and verbs. On the other hand, counter-evidence to this hypothesis would come from cases of bilingualism in which significant syntactic changes occur in the grammar of the two languages spoken by bilinguals despite a low frequency of interference in functional features. There was no evidence of such cases in the data discussed in this book.

It might also be the case that a common specification of features for equivalent functional categories is developed for both languages such that, whereas in monolingual varieties of the two languages two clearly distinct sets of features are associated with the same functional category, in bilingual varieties a common set of features is associated with the same functional category. In those cases, a fusion of feature specifications takes place. I will refer to the results of this fusion as convergence. If the feature specification of functional categories is part of the lexicon and if access to both languages is frequent among bilinguals living in a language contact situation, as exemplified by code-mixing, then one would expect long-term effects of interference on the functional features in both languages. If language A encodes distinctions that pertain to intrinsic features such as person or gender differently from language B, then constant access to the two lexicons might yield the results of convergence in one particular set of values for the same functional category. Thus, convergence is the specification of a common set of features for a functional category for both languages. This proposal is more specific than previous notions of convergence because functional convergence is understood as a mechanism used by bilinguals in a language-contact situation to select, from a large set of possible values for functional features that are compatible with the linguistic input, a common set of functional features related to a specific functional head in the two languages.

In order to begin an exploration of the linguistic factors that render functional convergence possible, I propose the following hypothesis:

Functional Convergence Hypothesis
Convergence, the specification of a common set of features shared by the equivalent functional categories in the two languages spoken by a bilingual individual, takes place when a set of features that is not activated in language A is frequently activated by input in language B in the bilingual mind. Convergence may be the result of the fusion of features associated with a functional category in language A with other features associated with that category in language B or, in certain cases, it may be the result of the emergence of a new functional category in one of the languages that is not present in the syntactic representation of monolingual speakers of that language.

This hypothesis states that, when convergence takes place, it results from frequent activation of features not shared by the two languages. The data discussed in this book will provide support for the notion that interference and convergence are more likely to take place in features that are affected by constant activation in discourse. Those are functional features that are crucial for the interpretation of the informational structure of the sentence and that relate antecedents across discourse. A proposal that targets features involved in discourse interpretation has been by made by Sorace (2000, 2003) to account for incomplete specification of sentential subjects in L2 near-native grammars and for attrition in the L1 grammars of near native L2 speakers. In this book, I will focus on convergence in features associated with the direct object system not as an instantiation of unattained grammars or language loss, but as a mechanism that accounts for fusion in functional categories and for the emergence of new functional categories in second-generation bilinguals in a language contact situation. The Functional Convergence Hypothesis predicts that, when convergence takes place, it is found in those cases of bilingualism in which equivalent categories have different sets of features associated with them in the two languages spoken by the bilingual and are constantly activated in discourse. In this book, evidence in favor of convergence in functional features will be presented based on data from bilinguals living in a contact situation who have access to input in the two languages in their communities and at home and for whom some evidence of code-mixing can be found. The data indicate a common specification of interpretable features in clitic pronouns and null objects as well as evidence in favor of positing a common specification for the functional projection Clitic Phrase for Quechua and Spanish that results in a common SVO word order for both languages.

Cases in which convergence has taken place despite low levels of activation of dissimilar sets of features in the two languages spoken by the bilingual will be counter-evidence to this hypothesis. In analyzing the interpretable functional features related to the pronominal system and to the determiner system in the data presented in this book no such evidence was found.

CHAPTER 2

The direct object system of Quechua and Spanish

Direct objects have traditionally been analyzed as complements of the verb in the VP-internal position closest to the verb in X′-Theory (Jackendoff 1977). This internal position has also been linked to the their thematic properties. As themes, they have been identified as the lowest elements in a thematic hierarchy and this position correlates with the most internal position inside the verbal phrase (VP) in an X′-theoretical approach (Baker 1988, Grimshaw 1990). In such syntactic representations, direct objects received Case as internal arguments of verbs through the Government relationship (Chomsky 1986b). In the early Minimalist Approach (Chomsky 1993), an attempt was made to unify Case assignment under the Spec–Head relationship and the functional category Object Agreement (AgrO) was posited as the locus where the phi-features of direct objects were checked and where Case was assigned to the direct object. In later versions, for example, in Chomsky (1995), the status of the AgrO projection has become more dubious, as there is no interpretive motivation for it. Direct objects are treated as complements of the lower verb V. The determiner features (D-features) in the verb motivate their movement.

2.1 Functional features in the direct object system

From a distributional perspective, languages differ with respect to the position of the object as pre-verbal or post-verbal. In theoretical models that do not posit an AgrO projection, this difference has been treated as a parametric difference in the directionality of the Head-Parameter (Koopman 1984, Travis 1984). Languages with transitive verbs in final position, such as Quechua, have been treated as involving a Complement-Verb word order, as illustrated by the following examples from Ulcumayo Quechua and Lamas Quechua:[1]

Northern Junín (Ulcumayo) Quechua
(1) Wamra alqu-ta apa-ya-n.
 boy dog-ACC bring-DUR-3SG
 'The boy brings the dog' (Black, Bolli and Ticsi 1990)

Lamas Quechua
(2) Pay yaku-ta apa-yka-n.
 he water-ACC bring-DUR-3SG
 'He brings water' (Coombs, Coombs and Weber 1976)[2]

Languages that place direct objects in sentence-final positions have been analyzed as having a Verb-Complement word order. One of such languages is Spanish:

San Juan (Subject SJ 29)
(3) Después el niño ha cargado la ranita.
 then the boy has carried the froggy
 'Then the boy picked up the froggy'

One of the main problems with the head-parameter hypothesis is cross-linguistic variation in the directionality of lexical and functional heads. In Quechua, fronting of a direct object wh-word is usually accompanied by verb-movement to a higher left position, as evidenced by the final position of the subject, exemplified by the following wh-question taken from a Northern Junín Quechua grammar text:

Northern Junín Quechua (Ulcumayo Quechua)
(4) ¿Ima-ta-m willapa-nakaraa-ri-n wak awkin-kuna?
 what-ACC-FOC tell-RECIPR-PAST-3SG DEM senior-PL
 'What did those old persons tell each other?'
 (Black, Bolli and Ticsi Zarate 1990. p. 166)

If the verb moves as a head, it does so to a position that is probably higher than V and to the left of it. In principle, nothing precludes Quechua from having different parametric values for the lexical head V and for functional projections.

---

1. I assume that these declarative sentences represent the canonical word order in both languages, that is, a word order that is not affected by focusing a particular constituent in the sentence.

2. Coombs, Coombs and Weber's (1976) example has a locative. Although they give SOV as the canonical word order in San Martin (Lamas) Quechua, they do not provide an example with only these three constituents.

Nevertheless, the motivation for such variation remains puzzling. In the literature, other proposals have been made to unify such asymmetries in the directionality of the head parameter across categories.

In Kayne's (1995) proposal, parametric variation between the two languages follows from the availability of movement. All languages are assumed to have an initial Specifier-Head-Complement (SVO) word order and variations are due to verb movement and XP-movement. In minimalist models, the differences in the strength of the D-feature in V are responsible for variation in direct object movement that yields differences in word order.

Whether one adopts a head-parameter, a Kaynian or a minimalist perspective, the presence of interference in word order in bilinguals could be tested by changes in word order in declarative sentences with transitive verbs. However, the distribution of word order in Quechua and Spanish is complicated by other possible word orders in addition to the canonical ones that encode differences in the topic/focus structure of the sentence. Some of those word orders involve constituent and verb movement as suggested by the fact that the subject remains in the lowest position:

Lamas Quechua
(5) Chayrayku wañu-chi-n   killa-ta-ka   inti-ka.
    then   kill-CAUS-3SG moon-ACC-TOP sun-TOP
    'Then, the sun kills the moon'
    (Coombs, Coombs and Weber 1976 p. 162)

Ulcumayo Quechua
(6) Rantiku-rka-n-mi pitasulampaqa rasyun-ni-n-ta   michiqkuna.
    sell-PAST-3SG-FOC pieces   portion-EUPHONIC-3SG-ACC shepherds
    'The shepherds sell parts of their portions'
    (Black, Bolli and Ticsi Zarate 1990 p. 58)

Spanish
(7) Está buscando una secretaria el jefe   de   fábrica.
    is   looking for a secretary the foreman of   the factory
    'The factory's foreman is looking for a secretary' (Zubizarreta 1998 p. 126)

In these sentences, the canonical word order is altered in order to focalize subcomponents of the sentence, although not necessarily with the same interpretive results. I will elaborate on these differences later. For the moment, what is relevant to our argumentation is the availability, in both languages, of verb and constituent movement to the left in order to express different topic/focus information. Thus, in examining possible interference concerning direct objects in both languages it is crucial to look beyond VP and to identify higher projections that are involved in verb and argumental XP-movement driven by the focus/topic structure of the sentence (Rizzi 1997).

Changes in word order that are driven by the informational structure of the sentence are associated in Quechua, but not in Spanish, to discourse particles, mostly topic and focus or evidentiality markers. These are suffixes that may be added to an inflected noun or verb. The topic marker for Ulcumayo Quechua is -*qa* or its variant -*ga* and for Lamas Quechua -*ka*. Both markers, when attached to an argument, are used to signal a change in discourse topic.[3] The following examples from narratives in the two varieties of Quechua illustrate this property:

Ulcumayo Quechua
(8) Chawra-**qa** rirka-naka-raa-ri-n-shi   kuntur-wan atuq-**qa**.
    then-TOP   see-RECIPROCAL-PL-PAST-3SG-REPORT condor-CONJ fox-TOP
    'And then, the condor and the fox saw each other (they say)'

(9) Kuntur-**qa** taya-n-shi.
    condor-TOP seat-3SG-REPORT
    'And the condor sat down (they say)' (Black, Bolli and Ticsi 1990 p. 165)

Lamas Quechua
(10) Killa-**ka**   yaku.
     moon-TOP water
     'The moon is water'

(11) Inti-**ka**   nina.
     sun-TOP fire
     'The sun is fire'

(12) *Siempre*, inti-shi   wañu-chi-n   killa-ta-**ka**   nina-wan.
     always   sun-REPORT kill-CAUS-3SG moon-ACC-TOP fire-INSTR
     '(That is why) the sun always kills the moon with fire (they say)'
     (Coombs, Coombs and Weber 1976 p. 162)

In addition to topic marking, for each variety of Quechua there is a three-way distinction in evidentiality: first hand information, hearsay and doubt. The following table presents the suffixes and their meaning in the two varieties of

---

3. For Lamas Quechua, Coombs, Coombs and Weber (1976) identify other functions such as a change of role in discourse. In this study, I will focus on its function as the marker of a new topic.

Table 1. Evidentiality markers in Quechua

Evidentiality value	Ulcumayo Quechua	Lamas Quechua
First hand or affirmative	-mi, -m	-mi, -m
Second hand or reportative	-shi, -sh	-shi, -sh
Dubitative	-tru, -tr	-cha

Quechua. (There are no distinctions in the meaning of these suffixes in the two varieties under study.)

The suffixes can be added to main verbs, arguments and adverbial expressions. In addition to their evidentiality values they also carry a focalizing force. The following examples from Ulcumayo Quechua illustrate their uses (Black, Bolli and Ticsi Zarate 1990 p. 72):

(13) Kaya-n-**mi** sanurya.
 be-3SG-FOC carrots
 'There ARE carrots'

(14) Huk hunaq-**shi** pukla-shun.
 one day-REPORT play-1PL.INCHOATIVE
 'We will play ONE DAY (they say)'

(15) Pay rura-nqa-**tr**.
 he do-3-SG.FUT-DUB
 '(I doubt) he will DO it'

In sentence (13) the particle *-mi* asserts the attested value of the evidential marker and focalizes the event referred to by the verb that is interpreted as new information. In sentence (14), the DP *Huk hunaq* 'one day' is marked with a reportative value and appears in fronted position and also marked as new information. Finally, in sentence (15) the verb is marked for a dubitative value of the evidentiality paradigm.

There are also other discourse-related particles such as the limitative *-la* in Ulcumayo and *-lla* in Lamas Quechua and the emotive suffix *-yu* in Ulcumayo and *-ya* in Lamas. Limitative *-la* or *-lla* is used to express a meaning close to *only* in English:

 Ulcumayo Quechua
(16) Alqu-**la** puri-ya-n.
 dog-LIMIT walk-DUR-3SG
 'Only the dog is walking'

Emotive -*yu* or -*ya* are used to express positive and negative emotions such as pain, sadness, happiness and rage. The sentence comes from a context in which the speaker is evoking her dead younger sister.

Lamas Quechua
(17) Chasnami-**ya**   pay-ka rima-rka-n.
    that way-EMOTIVE she-TOP speak-PAST-3SG
    'She spoke that way' (Coombs, Coombs and Weber 1976 p. 155)

Another important variable that must be considered when looking at potential cross-linguistic interference in the direct object system of Quechua-Spanish bilinguals is the contrast in case marking. In Quechua overt direct objects receive an accusative case- marking morpheme as illustrated in sentences (18) and (19). I will discuss some of the properties that make -*ta* an accusative marker as well as other specific properties that may indicate that this suffix is in the process of extending its properties beyond accusative case marking.

Traditional Quechua grammars include the suffix -*ta* as a morpheme that is used to mark accusative case on direct objects as shown by the following examples from Lamas and Ulcumayo Quechua:

Lamas Quechua
(18) Aycha-ta-mi   ranti-ra-ni.
    meat-ACC-FOC buy-PAST-1SG
    'I bought meat' (Coombs, Coombs and Weber 1976, p. 88)

Ulcumayo Quechua
(19) Pay alqu-ta maqa-ya-n.
    he dog-ACC beat-DUR-3SG
    'S/he is beating the dog' (Balck, Bolli and Ticsi Zarate 1990, p. 48)

However, in certain cases, the same marker is used to mark other internal arguments of the verb such as indirect objects, as shown in (20), or even some adjuncts, in particular those that indicate the goal of a movement verb as shown in (21):

(20) Pedru-ka peluta-ta Juan-ta   ku-rka-n.
    Pedru-TOP ball-ACC Juan-DAT give-PAST-3SG
    'Pedro gave the ball to Juan' (Coombs, Coombs and Weber 1976, p. 88)

(21) Allin-ta-chu puñu-nkichis.
    good-ACC-Q sleep-2PL
    'Did you sleep well?'

Van de Kerke (1996), in his discussion of Bolivian Quechua, considers these as cases in which -*ta* corresponds to structural objective case. "Structural objective case is assigned by the verb to any constituent in the government domain of that head (VP)" (Van de Kerke 1996, p. 93). Accusative case is a subset of objective case. For Van de Kerke, "accusative case, -*ta*, is assigned by a verb to its immediate sister (the object or direct argument)" (Van de Kerke, 1996, p. 93). One of the arguments that he provides for such a distinction is the fact that it is clear that the intransitive verb in (21) cannot assign accusative case to the adverbial expression. Therefore, he concludes, the adverbial expression is marked with objective but not accusative case. This property of the morpheme -*ta* will be later referred to in the analysis of the loss of the morphological marker in Bilingual Quechua.

There are other properties of the accusative marker -*ta* that correspond to the properties of definite determiners and partially to those of the preposition *a* in Spanish. Determiners are null in Quechua in DPs in all positions,[4] but they are overt in Spanish in subject position, and in object position they are overt when they are non-generic, as illustrated by the following example:

(22) María tiene *(la/una) moneda.
 María has *(the/a) coin
 'María has the/a coin'

In Spanish, determiners also license null nouns in expressions of the following type:

(23) Compr-é la roja.
 bought-1SG.PAST the red
 'I bought the red (one)'

The accusative marker -*ta* in Quechua has been proposed to act as a licenser of null nouns in direct object position (Mark Baker pc) as in the following example:[5]

---

4. The language does have demonstratives as in:
(i) Mariya **chay** papa-ta apa-ru-n.
 Mariya that potato-ACC bring-PAST-3SG
 'Mariya brought that potato'

5. This is part of a debate between Wilhelm Adelaar and David Weber on whether Quechua distinguishes between adjectives and nouns (Mark Baker p.c.).

(24) Puka-**ta** ranti-rka-ni.
    red-ACC buy-PAST-1SG
    'I bought the red one'

If the accusative marker does license a null noun, then it behaves as the definite determiner in English (Mark Baker p.c.) or in Spanish. Its licensing capabilities in Quechua, however, are more extended than those of the Spanish determiner, as it licenses extraction of adjectival modifiers out of DP in topicalizations as in (25):

(25) Hatun-**ta** rirka-ra-ni   wasi-ta.
    big-ACC see-PAST-1SG house-ACC
    'I saw a big house'

This is a property not shared by the Spanish definite determiner:

(26) *La roja vi la casa.
     the red saw the house
     'I saw a red house'

Thus, if there are similarities between the Spanish definite determiner and the Quechua accusative marker -*ta*, these are only partial, and it is not easy to attribute them to clearly identifiable functional features. Some of these similarities will be taken into account when discussing the evidence in favor of convergence in the functional features of determiners in Quechua and Spanish bilingual grammars.

Besides determiners, the only other candidate for interference in case marking is the preposition *a* in Spanish that precedes animate and specific direct objects:

(27) Vi a María / *a los libros.
    saw to María / *to the books
    '(I) saw María/the books'

However, such level of specificity is not found in Quechua accusative marking, which is, depending on the context, compatible with definite, indefinite or generic interpretations:

(28) Papa-**ta**   ranti-rka-ni.
    potato-ACC buy-PAST-1SG
    'I bought (a/the) potato (es)'

Finally, the fact that both languages are null subject languages with rich overt subject morphology and complex direct object morphology is itself important

Table 2. Subject agreement in Northern Junín (Ulcumayo) Quechua and Lamas Quechua

Ulcumayo Quechua	Lamas Quechua	Person and number features
Kaya-: '(I) am'	Ri-**ni** '(I) go'	1p sg
Kaya-**nki** 'You are'	Ri-**nki** 'You go'	2p sg
Kaya-**n** 'He is'	Ri-**n** 'He goes'	3p sg
Ka-rka-**yaa:** 'We are (exclusive)'	Ri-**ni-sapa** 'We go (exclusive)'	1p pl exclusive
Kaya-**nchi** be-1PL 'We are (inclusive)'	Ri-**nchi** 'We go (inclusive)'	1p pl inclusive
Ka-rka-**ya-nki** be-PL-DUR-2 'You are pl.'	Ri-**nkichi** 'You go'	2p pl
Ka-rka-**ya-n** be-PL-DUR-3 'They eat'	Ri-**n**(sapa) 'They go'	3p pl

to take into account when looking at interference in bilinguals. Quechua and Spanish have overt subject morphology in the form of verb suffixes. The paradigm is more transparent in Quechua as subject person morphology is not fused with tense or aspect, and in some cases it is distinct from number, as shown by the paradigms in Table 2 from Ulcumayo Quechua (Black, Bolli and Ticsi 990) and Lamas Quechua (Coombs, Coombs and Weber 1976).

In both varieties of Quechua the past tense is marked with an independent morpheme as shown in the following examples:

Ulcumayo Quechua
(29) Miku-**ru**-n.
 eat-PAST-3SG
 '(S/he) ate'

Lamas Quechua
(30) Miku-**rka**-n.
 eat-PAST-3SG
 '(S/he) ate'

In Spanish the paradigm is more complex because person morphemes are fused with tense as shown by the following examples from past tense.

Table 3. Subject agreement in standard Peruvian Spanish[6,7]

Compr-é 'I bought'	1p sg past
Compr-aste 'You bought'	2p sg past
Compr-ó 'S/he bought'	3p sg past
Compr-amos 'We bought'	1p pl past
Compr-aron 'They bought'	3p pl past

Object agreement in Quechua is quite complex. It is encoded in synthetic morphemes that include subject and object markings for first person subject/second person object, first person subject/third person object and second person subject/third person object. In some cases, morphemes that are used for first person subject with intransitive verbs may be used to encode third person subjects when combined with a first person object morpheme (see below). In Ulcumayo Quechua, insertion of the plural morpheme *-yaa* produces ambiguous readings. In Lamas Quechua, ambiguous readings arise in first person plural objects and third and second person subjects. What is crucial for our study on language interference and convergence is that for both varieties of Quechua, the only cases in which no overt object morpheme can be found is for third person subject/third person object. Also very important to our study is the fact that object agreement in Quechua does not encode gender, definiteness or specificity and there is not an independent series of morphemes that mark dative case on verbs, which would be analogous to dative clitics. The paradigms for Ulcumayo Quechua and Lamas Quechua are presented in Tables 4 and 5.

Some researchers have favored the view that Spanish has an object agreement system encoded as accusative clitics or weak pronouns (Suñer 1988, Franco 1993, Everett 1996). If clitics are indeed agreement morphemes, they are prefixes or suffixes marked for case, gender, number, definiteness and specificity values. Unlike in Quechua, in Spanish subject and object agreement are independent and the third person direct object agreement morphemes are overt.[8] There is also variation across dialects in the cliticization of direct objects. While some varieties of Spanish use accusative clitic forms marked for gender such as *lo(s)*, *la(s)*, others use the dative clitics *le(s)* marked only for

---

6. This past tense is not frequently used by Quechua-Spanish bilinguals presumably due to its lack of an epistemic value in Bilingual Spanish (Escobar 1994b).

7. I do not include the 2nd person plural that is used only in Peninsular Spanish.

8. Changes in morphosyntactic word order do arise in the combination of accusative and dative morphology (Bonet 1995) and certain logical orders are proscribed.

Table 4. Object agreement in Ulcumayo Quechua

Verb form	Person paradigm
Wiya-**q** 'I hear you'	2p sg object — 1p sg subject
Wiya-**maa-nki** 'You hear me'	1p sg object — 2p sg subject
Wiya-**maa-n** 'S/he hears me'	1p sg object — 3p sg subject
Wiya-**maa-nchi** 'S/he hears us'	1p pl incl object — 3p sg subject
Wiya-**shunki** 'S/he hears you'	2p pl object — 3p sg subject
Wiya-**yaq** 'We/I hear you'	2p sg/pl object — 1p sg/pl (excl) subject
Wiya-**yaa-ma-n** 'They hear me'	1p sg object — 3p pl subject
'S/he hears us'	1p pl excl object — 3p sg subject
'They hear us'	1p pl excl object — 3p pl subject
Wiya-**yaa-ma-nki** 'You hear me'	1p sg object — 2p pl subject
'You hear us'	1p pl incl object — 2p sg subject
Wiya-**yaa-shunki** 'They hear you'	2p sg object — 3p pl subject
'S/he hears you'	2p pl object — 3p sg subject
	2p pl object — 3p pl subject

(Black, Bolli and Ticsi 1990)

Table 5. Object agreement in Lamas Quechua

Verb form	Person paradigm
Maka-**yki** 'I hit you'	2p sg object — 1p sg subject
Maka-**wa-nki** 'You hit me'	1p sg object — 2p sg subject
Maka-**wa-n** 'S/he hits me'	1p sg object — 3p sg subject
Maka-**wa-n-sapa-nchi** 'S/he hits us'	1p pl incl object — 3p sg subject
'They hit us'	1 p pl incl object — 3p pl subject
Maka-**shu-nki** 'S/he hits you'	2p sg object — 3p sg subject
Maka-**yki-chi** 'I hit you'	2p pl object — 1p sg subject
Maka-**wa-n-sapa** 'They hit me'	1p sg object — 3p pl subject
'S/he hit us'	1p pl excl object — 3p sg subject
'They hear us'	1p pl excl object — 3p pl subject
Maka-**wa-nkichi** 'You hit me'	1p sg object — 2p pl subject
Maka-**wa-nki-sapa** 'You hit us'	1p pl object — 2p sg subject
Maka-**shunki-sapa** 'They hit you'	2ps object — 3p pl subject
Maka-**shunki-chi** 'S/he/They hit you'	2p pl object — 3p sg subject
	2p pl object — 3p pl subject
Maka-**nki-chi** 'You hit him/them'	3p sg/pl object — 2p sg subject
Maka-**ni-sapa** 'We (excl) hit him/them'	3p sg/pl object — 1p pl excl subject
Maka-**nchi** 'We (incl) hit him/them'	3p sg/pl object — 1p pl incl subject

(Coombs, Coombs and Weber 1976)

Table 6. Direct object and subject agreement paradigms in standard Peruvian Spanish

Direct Object clitics	Subject agreement	Person paradigm
Me	Veo	1p sg
Te	Ves	2p sg
Lo/la/le/se	Ve	3p sg m/f
Nos	Vemos	1p pl
Los/las/se	Ven	2/3p pl

number. These uses vary according to the verb used and to variables such as animacy, mass/count distinctions and pragmatic functions in discourse.[9]

The standard paradigm for present tense used in Peru is shown in Table 6.

To summarize, I have presented syntactic and morphological phenomena in Quechua and Spanish that must be taken into account in order to analyze language interference in bilinguals. These are canonical word order, changes in word order driven by changes in information structure that are associated with discourse-related morphology, the partially similar functions of Quechua accusative case marking and Spanish determiners, and verbal subject and object agreement morphology.

Given these general characteristics of the two languages under study, I will focus on interference or convergence of functional features in three types of structures:

1. Sentences with overt direct objects within neutral information structures (canonical word orders).
2. Sentences with fronted direct objects and their relationship to direct object agreement morphology, case marking, and discourse particles.
3. Sentences with null objects.

---

9. The bibliography on clitics is abundant. For a recent overview on dialectal variation in the use of clitic forms see Camacho and Sanchez (2002).

2.2 The direct object system of Quechua: Word order and pronominalization

2.2.1 Canonical word order in Quechua

One of the most important aspects determining the differentiation between a language's canonical word order and other possible word orders is the availability of verb movement. In minimalist proposals, transitive verbs involve a lower VP and a higher vP (Chomsky 1995). Direct objects are generated as sisters to V in a VP-internal position and check accusative features in the specifier of the lower VP. If the general analysis of transitive verbs is correct, Quechua direct objects also move to the specifier of the VP. The question is whether there is overt verb movement to a higher position outside VP. This question is of particular importance because Quechua has complex overt subject agreement morphology that is assumed to involve strong features that force movement to Tense or Agreement functional heads.

One traditional test for verb movement is the relative position of adverbs. In the two varieties of Quechua analyzed in this study, adverbs tend to be suffixes on the verb, but there is a manner adverb that can be used for testing. The adverb *allin* "well" is pre-verbal in sentences with a canonical word order:[10]

(31) **Allin**-ta papa-ta miku-n.
well-ACC potato-ACC eat-3SG
'(S/he) eats potatoes well'

The adverb may appear after the verb only in sentences in which a pause precedes it:

(32) Papa-ta miku-n # **allin**-ta.
potato-ACC eat-3SG well-ACC
'(S/he) eats potatoes well'

I take this to indicate that in Quechua, the verb remains inside the VP in sentences with canonical SOV word order such as sentences (1) and (2). These sentences have the structure in (33):[11]

---

10. These sentences were tested with an adult Quechua-Spanish bilingual speaker from Ulcumayo.
11. I assume here Koopman and Sportiche's (1988) VP-internal subject hypothesis.

(33)

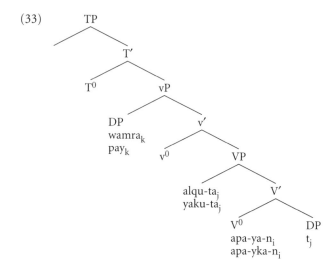

In this structure the subject is generated in the specifier of the higher vP layer as in Chomsky (1995) and the direct object checks its features through Spec–Head agreement with the verb by moving to the specifier of the lower VP. The verb remains inside the VP. It is possible for the subject to remain inside the VP, in which case it receives nominative case through the AGREE relationship (Chomsky 1998) by checking its case features against those of T, assuming T acts as a probe that checks nominative case. It could also be the case that when the subject is the topic of the sentence it raises to the Spec of higher projection, either Spec of TP or Spec of CP. Sentences with canonical word order do not provide evidence for further movement of the subject.

The lack of verb movement to T in canonical word order does not preclude the possibility of movement to T or C in other types of sentences due to evidentiality and focus reasons.[12] In Quechua, it is possible to have verbs in initial positions followed by an evidentiality/focus particle as in the affirmative sentence in example (6). I would like to propose that in those cases the verb has moved to a higher CP position in order to satisfy or check focus features

---

12. I follow Zubizarreta's (1998) proposal according to which verbs can constitute focalized constituents. They can be identified as the answer to a wh-question, assuming that the answer has the same presuppositions as the question. The following question-answer pair illustrates a case in which the verb is focalized in English:
(i) What did John do with the pie?
(ii) [John] [[$_F$ ate] the pie]] (Zubizarreta 1998 p. 3)

(Zagona 2002). This CP position is not projected in canonical sentences; this assumption is based on Grimshaw's (1994) notion of Minimal Projection, according to which projections are legitimate only when they are motivated.

2.2.2 Fronted direct objects

Having proposed a structure for sentences with canonical SOV word order in Quechua, I turn now to the other possible word orders. Direct object fronting or scrambling is possible in Quechua yielding OVS and OSV word orders, as attested in many grammars of the Quechua language family (Cerrón-Palomino 1987). The following examples tested with bilingual speakers are consistent with descriptions of monolingual varieties:

Ulcumayo Quechua
(34) [[$_O$ Ishkay agash-ta-ga]   [$_V$ qipi-ru-n]]   [$_S$ chay wamra].
       two   frogs-ACC-TOP   carry-PAST-3SG   that boy
'The boy carried two frogs'

Lamas Quechua
(35) [[$_O$ Ishkay sapitu-ta-ka]   [$_V$ api-yka-n]]   [$_S$ kay wambriyo].
       two   toads-ACC-TOPIC   hold-DUR-3SG   this boy
'The boy is holding two toads'

These sentences are felicitous in the following context: My interlocutor and I are in an environment where frogs or toads are very important and have been previously mentioned in discourse. I see a child leaving the area carrying something. I ask my interlocutor what happened, and I get the responses in (34) and (35) for each variety of Quechua. In these sentences the DP "two frogs" or "two toads" are in a topic position and the verb is new information or focus. The DP "that/this boy" is contextual information but is not the topic of the conversation. For such sentences, I propose the representation in (36) that has two functional projections higher than TP. These are Topic Phrase (TopP) and Focus Phrase (FocP):[13]

---

13. Functional projections related to the informational structure of the clause have been proposed by many authors before, among them Uriagereka (1995) and Rizzi (1997).

(36)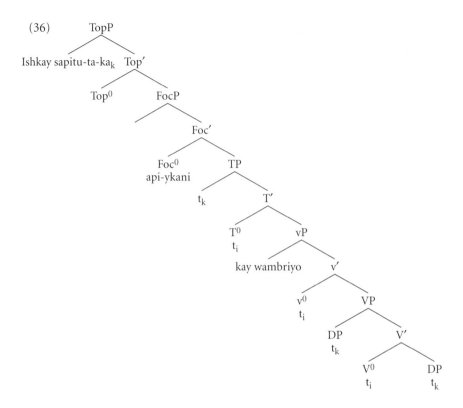

In this representation, the order OVS is derived from SOV by V movement to the head of FocP. The direct object moves from its VP-internal position to a higher spec of Topic position, as evidenced by the possibility of reconstruction:

(37) Wawa-n_i-kuna-ta   rirkayan lapan   mama-kuna$_i$.
     child-POSS3$_i$-PL-ACC saw   all/each mama-PL$_i$
     'All/each mother(s) saw their/her children'

In this sentence, the quantified expression *lapan mamakuna* 'each mother' binds the NP *wawa-n-kuna-ta* 'her children'. Such an interpretation is possible because the NP reconstructs back to its original position inside the VP. Movement of the verb does not violate any minimality constraints as it proceeds regularly from head to head. Movement of the direct object crosses over the subject in Spec of the higher VP. No minimality effects arise either because this movement is motivated to satisfy a [+topic] feature for which the subject is not marked.

According to an adult informant from Ulcumayo, the word order OSV is used in contexts in which the topic of previous discourse is the direct object but the sentence is not an answer to the question of what happened, as in (38) (the suffix *-ga* is required in discourse) and (39):

Ulcumayo Quechua
(38) (Chaypita) agash-ta-(ga)   tortuga qipi-ru-n.
     (then)   frog-ACC-(TOPIC) turtle   carry-PAST-3SG
     'And then the turtle carried the frog'

Lamas Quechua
(39) Kay sapitu-ta-ka   tortuga miku-naya-yka-n.
     this frog-ACC-TOPIC turtle eat-REPET-PROGR-3SG
     'The turtle is eating this frog'

In these sentences the verb is not focused, does not move outside the VP, and, presumably, the direct object topic is base generated in the specifier of Topic position, as illustrated in (40):

(40)
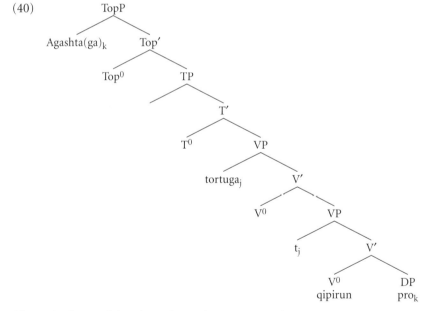

Evidence in favor of the object being base generated in a Topic position is the less acceptable reconstruction in (41), with a bound interpretation for the noun phrase **wawa-n-kuna-ta** 'their children':

(41) ??Wawa-n$_i$-kuna-ta   lapan   warmikuna$_i$ rikayan.
     child-POSS3$_i$-PL-ACC all/each woman-PL$_i$ saw
     'All/each mothers saw their children'

These representations show that in Quechua fronted objects may be the result of movement or may be base generated. Notice however, that in Quechua object fronting, such as the one represented in (36), does not require any object agreement morphology on the verb. In the analysis of the bilingual data, this will be considered an important difference with respect to the grammar of Spanish and it will have some bearing on the explanation of how interference and convergence in functional features yield different possibilities for word order in the bilingual grammar.

2.2.3 Fronted verbs

Finally, I will address verb-initial word orders in Quechua. VSO word orders occur with an independent particle on the verb that is used to mark focus and evidentiality as previously discussed and shown in (42):

Ulcumayo Quechua
(42) Upya-ru-n-mi wamra yaku-ta.
    drink-PAST-3SG-FOC boy water-ACC
    'The boy DRANK the water'

In this sentence the verb moves for evidentiality/focus reasons, as supported by the use of the suffix -*mi*. There is no indication of subject or object movement so it is safe to assume that the subject remains in Spec of vP and the object remains in spec of the lower VP:

(43)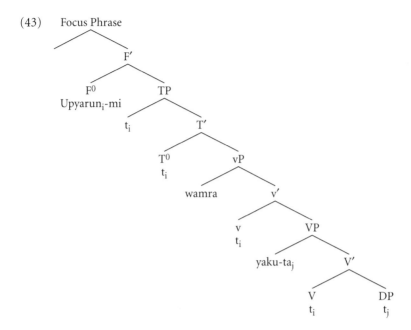

According to one of my informants, a native speaker of Ulcumayo Quechua, there is another possibility for verb fronting that is accompanied by a focus marker on the object as in the following sentence:

Ulcumayo Quechua
(44) Upya-ru-n   wamra yaku-ta-m.
     drink-PAST-3SG boy   water-ACC-FOC
     'The boy drank the water'

This sentence can be uttered if the boy and the water are salient in the speaker and the hearer's mind. The following is a context in which it is felicitous: there are two adults and a boy in a room. In the room there is a container of water that is important to the adults. The two adults have been observing the child as he plays around with different objects in the room. One of the adults leaves the room for a couple of seconds and upon returning finds the other adult upset. She then asks: *Ima pasarun?* 'What happened?' The other adult replies using sentence (44). I propose that, in this case, the verb is focused as it represents new information, but the constituent "the water", despite being background information, receives some form of in-situ contrastive focus.

Despite the fact that the grammars usually mention all word orders as possible in Quechua, I could not find an example of VOS word order in the grammars of Northern Junín (Ulcumayo) Quechua. In my corpus there was only one such case and it involved a Spanish verb complete with Spanish verbal morphology:

Ulcumayo Quechua
(45) Van viendo caja-ta   niño, tortuga, algu.
      go looking box-ACC boy   turtle   dog
      'The boy, the turtle and the dog are looking at the box'

For Lamas Quechua I was able to find such word order in Coombs, Coombs and Weber (1976) but, as I will show in Chapter 4, it was not very frequent in the children's data.

Lamas Quechua
(46) Wañu-chi-n   killa-ta-ka   inti-ka.
      die-CAUS-3SG moon-ACC-TOP sun-TOP
      'The sun kills the moon'

These cases are difficult to analyze; in particular, the Lamas example involves a topic marker on the direct object and one on the subject. Clearly, the verb raises to the Focus Phrase; however, in order to account for the direct object position, an additional intervening functional projection is required with its specifier as the landing site for the direct object. This scrambling analysis has been proposed for VOS word orders in Spanish by Ordoñez (1998) based on evidence from Principle C effects, quantifier binding and reconstruction effects. Principle C effects in Quechua cannot be easily tested, as third person overt pronouns are either focused (see below) or topics. Quantifier binding and reconstruction effects obtain, indicating that there is an intermediate landing position.

(47) Rikayan wawa-n-ta$_i$ lapan mama-n-kuna$_j$.
      saw   child-POSS3SG-ACC$_i$ each mother-3-PL$_j$
      'All/each mother(s) saw her child'

The direct object in these sentences could move to the specifier of that intermediate position. There are two possible candidates for that position: TopP and TP. I will assume for the moment that the intermediate landing position is the specifier of TP. As previously mentioned, T in Quechua does not require V movement and spec of TP is not the locus of nominative case assignment.

All the previous examples show that, in Quechua, focus features motivate verb movement. As evidenced by the canonical SOV word order, verb movement does not appear to be motivated by T features nor by a category lower than focus.[14] The previous examples have also shown that when the verb moves for focus reasons, it is also possible for the object to move for topic reasons and be scrambled out of the VP. These facts will later on be related to object fronting possibilities in Spanish and their relationship to overt morphological markers on the verb and to the representation of direct objects in bilingual grammars.

2.2.4 Null D and strong pronouns

Another important morphosyntactic characteristic of the grammar of Quechua that is relevant to the discussion of the representation of the direct object system in bilinguals is the fact that Quechua has pronominal null objects. They are interpreted contextually or as referring to a topic previously introduced in discourse. The following discourse fragments from Ulcumayo and Lamas Quechua present exchanges between two speakers. In sentence (48), speaker A introduces the NP *chay sutukuna-ta* 'these drops' in discourse; in sentence (49), the demonstrative *kay-ta-qa* 'these ones' is used to refer back to that NP and in (50) a null object is used to refer to it:

Ulcumayo Quechua

(48) Chawra-qa rantika-yaa-ma-nki-man   chay **shutu-kuna-ta**$_i$.
     then-TOP sell-PL-1SG.OBJ-2SG.SUBJ-COND those drop-PL-ACC$_i$
     'Then could you sell me those drops?'

(49) Imanuypata **kay-ta-qa**$_i$ truraa-ku-shaq
     how   this-ACC-TOP$_i$ put-REFLEX-1SGFUT
     'How do I apply these?'

(50) Alita rura-shpti-qa, kima uura-ta-ra-n   e$_i$ shuya-nki.
     well do-SUBORD-TOP three hour-ACC-REP-FOC e$_i$ put-2SG
     'When they begin to work, put (them) on every three hours'
     (Boli and Ticsi Zarate 1990, p. 227–228)

A similar pattern can be found in the following fragment from Lamas Quechua. In sentence (51), the question introduces the noun root *aswaku* 'drink' modified

---

14. SVO word orders are possible but rare in monolingual Quechua and Cerrón-Palomino (1987) notes that VO word orders in subordinate structures are ungrammatical, as shown in:

(i) *[Miku-sqa-n-ta   tanta-ta]   yacha-ni.
    [eat-PAST-3SG-ACC bread-ACC] know-1SG
    'I know (that) you ate bread' (Cerrón-Palomino 1987, p. 290)

by deverbal morphology. The answer in (52) has a null object that refers to the direct object of the verb *upya-shka-nisapa* '(we) drank'. This indicates that the null object in discourse can have as its referent a noun root.

Lamas Quechua (adapted from Park and Wyss 1995, p. 16)
(51) **Aswaku**$_i$-shka-nkichi-chu?
chicha$_i$-PAST-2PL-INTERROG?
'Did you prepare chicha (a drink)?'

(52) Ari. **Aswaku**$_i$-shka-nisapa. Ñukñuk-puru-ta-mi   e$_i$ upya-shka-nisapa.
yes drink-PAST-1PL   sweet-INTENS-ACC-FOC e$_i$ drink-PAST-1PPL
'Yes, we prepared chicha. We drank (it) very sweet.'

By contrast, overt direct object pronouns are usually interpreted as focused elements as shown in the following pair of examples of overt pronouns and agreement morphology in Ulcumayo Quechua.[15] The overt pronoun in sentence (53) is interpreted as focalized although it does not require stress while the object agreement morphology in (54) is not interpreted in such a way:

Ulcumayo Quechua
(53) Pay qam-ta   maqa-shunki.
s/he you-ACC hits-OBJ2SG.SUBJ.3SG
'S/HE hits YOU'

(54) Maqa-shunki.
hits-2SG.OBJ.3SG.SUBJ
'S/he hits you'

This distinction will be relevant to the discussion of interference in the spell-out of pronominal forms in the grammar of bilingual children.

Finally, there is a contrast between Quechua and Spanish that is relevant to direct object complementation. Quechua direct object complement clauses are nominalized clauses as shown in (55) and cannot appear in isolation, as shown in (56):

(55) [Xwan-mi hamu-na-yki-ta]   yacha-rqa-n.
[Juan-FOC come-NOM-2S-ACC] know-PAST-3S
'Juan knew of your coming'
(example modified from Lefebvre and Muysken 1988, p. 240)

---

15. Parker (1976) gives this contrast for Anchas-Huailas Quechua, a variety very similar to Northern Junín Quechua.

(56) *Hamu-na-yki.
    come-NOM-2S
    'Your coming'

The suffix -*na* that appears in this subordinate clause is a nominalizing suffix that is followed by a nominal second person suffix. It provides information on tense that is relative to the main clause verbal tense but cannot occur or be interpreted independently from a main verb.

Spanish, on the other hand, has direct object clausal complements that have verb forms with tense information related to the main clause. Unlike in Quechua, these tense forms can occur in main clauses and can be interpreted in isolation, as shown in:

(57) María sabía que iba a venir.
    Maria knew that went to come
    'Maria knew that she was going to come'

(58) María iba a venir.
    Maria went to come
    'Maria was going to come'

I will assume, following Lefebvre and Muysken (1988), that T in Quechua subordinate clauses is a relative tense specified for +pronominal values while T in Spanish is a main tense not specified for pronominal values.

To summarize, in this subsection, I have presented evidence in favor of positing that in Quechua:

1. Canonical SOV word order is compatible with an analysis in which the subject, the verb and the object remain inside the VP.
2. OVS is derived from SOV via object movement to the spec of a Topic Phrase and verb movement to the head of a Focus Phrase. The subject remains in spec of the higher vP. OSV involves a representation in which the fronted object is based generated in spec of Topic Phrase, the subject and the verb are in VP.
3. For VSO, the verb moves to Focus, the subject and the object remain inside VP.
4. For VOS, the verb moves to Focus, the object moves to the Spec of TP.
5. Null pronouns are topic related.
6. Overt pronouns are focus related.
7. No overt agreement morpheme is required for third person objects.
8. Direct object complement clauses in Quechua have a [+pronominal] specification.

The statements in (1)–(4) converge on the idea that, in Quechua, the verb moves only for evidentiality or focus reasons and that verb movement is not required to satisfy T features. At the same time, the statements in (5)–(7) converge on the idea that agreement morphology and null pronouns are topic related in Quechua whereas overt pronouns are focus-related. Finally, statement (8) highlights the pronominal nature of subordinate tenses in Quechua.

2.3 The direct object system in Spanish: Word order and clitic-related constructions

2.3.1 Canonical word order in Spanish

SVO is the canonical word order in Spanish. It has been analyzed in the literature as involving verb movement (Suñer 1994) from its original VP-internal position to IP. Evidence in favor of this analysis comes from the post-verbal position of manner adverbs, as well as from question inversion (Zagona 2002 p. 166, 167):

(59) María leyó frecuentemente el diario.
 Maria read frequently the newspaper
 'Maria frequently read the newspaper'

(60) ¿Leyó Juan el diario?
 read Juan the newspaper
 'Did Juan read the newspaper?'

This analysis is compatible with the idea that direct objects move to the spec of the lower VP. In Spanish, objects raise to that position and verbs move to I^0 with the resulting VO word order (Suñer 1994). Ordoñez and Treviño (1999) have proposed that in sentences with overt subjects in Spanish, the subject is in the specifier of a higher Topic position. They point out that, in Spanish, structures containing overt subject DPs as well as fronted indirect and direct objects in Clitic Left Dislocation structures (CLLD) behave in a similar fashion with respect to ellipsis and quantifier and wh-extraction. Based on these similarities, they propose that, unlike null subjects which are pros in spec of TP, pre-verbal subject DPs are left-topicalized constituents in A′-positions, as shown in (61) and (62):

(61) Juan come papas.
 Juan eats potatoes
 'Juan eats potatoes'

(62)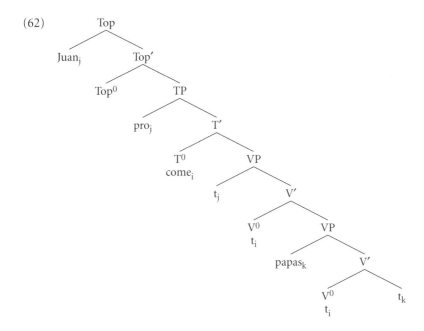

I will diverge somewhat from this analysis for Spanish SVO sentences but I will follow Ordoñez and Treviño's idea that they should be given the same analysis as CLLD constructions in light of their similar distribution. I will assume Sportiche's (1992, 1998) analysis for CLLD structures in Romance languages. It involves the projection of the functional category ClP. In this analysis, overt subjects in SVO constructions are in spec of Clitic Phrase (ClP). Zubizarreta (1998) has made a similar proposal for Spanish (see below). According to Zubizarreta, ClP is located between VP and TP. The head of this projection is not the clitic itself but an abstract operator "whose function is to ⟨⟨externalize⟩⟩ an argument of a verb v with respect to the tense associated with v" (Zubizarreta 1999, p. 256). In her view, "morphological identification of this head is achieved by a nominal morpheme with phi features contained within the local T. This may be a clitic or a strong agreement affix." (Zubizarreta 1999, p. 259). I will assume that morphological identification of the CL head is relevant to identify the features that trigger verb movement. In the ClP analysis of pre-verbal subjects, the verb moves to the head of ClP. Support for this movement comes from the relative position of manner adverbs.

(63) La viejita   compraba   frecuentemente   pan.
     the old lady bought   frequently   bread
     'The old lady often bought bread'

Thus, the structure for a sentence such as (63) is provided in (64):[16]

(64)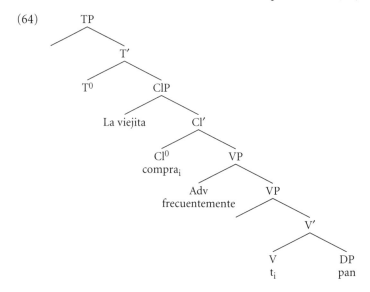

Thus, a major difference between Quechua and Spanish arises in this area of the syntax. Verbs move outside the VP in Spanish to Cl, a functional category associated with topic, while in Quechua verbs stay inside the VP in sentences with canonical word order and move only for focus reasons. What this implies for the syntactic representations of Quechua-Spanish bilinguals is that, if the Functional Interference Hypothesis is correct, interference in the functional features that trigger verb movement in the two languages will lead to a significant change in the syntax of either Quechua or Spanish with respect to their canonical word orders. Also, if there is constant activation of those features, the Functional Convergence Hypothesis predicts either a fusion of the functional features associated with verb movement in both languages such that focus or evidentiality features will be merged with the features that trigger verb movement in Spanish or the feature specification of Cl will emerge in Quechua. One would also expect that in cases in which interference or convergence do not take place, there are two representations available: one for Quechua SOV canonical word order in which the subject and the verb stay inside the VP and one for Spanish canonical SVO in which the verb moves at least to Cl and the subject moves to Spec of ClP.

---

16. For ease of exposition this representation does not include the VP-shell assumed previously.

2.3.2 Fronted direct objects and clitic-left dislocated structures

Unlike Quechua, Spanish has no morphological markers that indicate whether a constituent has been focused or topicalized. However, as proposed by Zubizarreta (1998) for Spanish, alterations in canonical word order are linked to the informational structure of the sentence. These emerge as a solution for a lack of correspondence between a phonological rule, the Nuclear Stress Rule (NSR)[17] and an interpretational rule, the Focus Prominence Rule (FPR). The NSR assigns more prominence to a node from a pair of metrical sisters that is lower in asymmetric c-command. The FPR states that given two constituents, one marked for focus and another not marked, the marked one is more prominent. This implies that the final constituent receives more prominence. However, if a constituent that is not generated in sentence-final position is marked for focus, prosody-motivated movement (p-movement) must take place in order to obtain a correspondence between NSR and FPR.

The consequence of this obligatory correspondence is that, if objects are not sentence-final, they cannot be interpreted as focused.[18] Their topic-related interpretation forces analyses in which they are base-generated or moved to a CP or TP-related position.

Based on a distinction originally proposed for Italian by Cinque (1990), Zubizarreta (1998) and Zagona (2002) distinguish between two types of fronted objects in Spanish: hanging topics (in Zubizarreta's terminology) or left-dislocated objects (in Zagona's) and CLLD structures. The two types differ with respect to their properties. The two contrasts relevant to this study are that, in structures with hanging topics but not in CLLD structures, the fronted object is external to the clause and it is not preceded by the preposition *a*. The following examples illustrate the two types:[19]

Hanging Topic
(65) Juan$_j$, lo$_i$ vimos   a él$_i$ en la fiesta.
     Juan$_j$ Cl$_i$ see-1PL.PAST to him$_i$ at the party
     'Juan, (we) saw him at the party'

---

17. Originally proposed for Romance languages by Cinque (1990)

18. They may still receive contrastive focus as defined by Zubizarreta (1998).

19. The different properties of the two types of constructions in Spanish are listed in Zagona (2002). These differences were first pointed out for Italian by Cinque (1990).

Clitic-left Dislocation
(66) A Juan$_i$ lo$_i$ vimos   en la fiesta.
      Juan$_i$ Cl$_i$ see-1PL.PAST at the party
      'Juan (we) saw him at the party'

Zubizarreta (1998) and Zagona (2002) propose different analyses for these two structures. Zagona (2002), assuming Rivero's (1980) and Hernanz and Brucart's (1987) analyses, proposes that hanging topics are base generated in the spec of Topic Phrase and are not related to clause-internal constituents. As hanging topics are not linked to agreement features in the sentence, I consider this analysis unproblematic and I will assume it in the following representation:

(67) [TopP DP [TP [VP [VP]]]]

Zubizarreta (1998) proposes that clause-internal discourse-related XPs such as topics or focalized constituents occupy the Spec of TP position. In her view, T is a syncretic category that may contain information about Tense and also about discourse-related features such as focus and topic. However, as mentioned before, for fronted objects in CLLD constructions, Zubizarreta (1998) proposes a different analysis. In CLLD structures, ClP is projected between TP and VP. Cl is a functional projection that attracts the object DP to its specifier position. This attraction is confirmed by the fact that definite direct objects in Spanish cannot be fronted without clitic doubling, irrespectively of the position of the subject, as shown by the following examples from Zubizarreta (1998):

(68) Esta ciudad$_i$ *(la$_i$)   destruyeron los bárbaros.
      this city   (Cl-ACC) destroyed   the barbarians
      'The barbarians destroyed this city' (Zubizarreta 1998, p. 110)
(69) Esta ciudad$_i$, los bárbaros   *(la$_i$)   destruyeron.
      this city   the barbarians (Cl-ACC) destroyed
      'The barbarians destroyed this city' (Zubizarreta 1998, p. 110)

In terms of their interpretation, I would like to point out that (68) is a felicitous answer to:

(70) ¿Quiénes destruyeron esta ciudad?
      'Who-PL destroyed this city?'

This indicates that in (68) the subject is new information, receives prominence, and is placed in sentence-final position in accordance to NSR.
   Sentence (69) is a felicitous answer to (71). In this sentence, the verb is new information, is more prominent, and is placed in sentence-final position.

(71) ¿Qué pasó con esta ciudad?
'What happened to this city?'

For sentences with OVS word orders, Zubizarreta (1998) proposes that the object is base-generated in Spec of ClP. She bases her proposal on the impossibility of reconstruction in restructuring structures:

(72) $^?$*El primer día de escuela, a su$_i$ hijo deberá acompañarlo$_i$
 the first day of school to her$_i$ child must accompany Cl-ACC$_i$
 cada madre$_i$.
 each mother$_i$
'Each mother must accompany her own child on the first day of school'
(example with glosses modified from Zubizarreta 1998, p. 115)

Sentence (72) shows that the direct object *a su hijo* 'her child" cannot be reconstructed to a VP-internal position. In the case of OSV sentences such as:

(73) A su propio hijo$_i$, ningún padre$_i$ lo$_i$ quiere castigar.
 to his own child no father Cl-ACC$_i$ wants to punish
'No father want to punish his own child'

the direct object is in a position higher than Spec of T and the subject QP *ningún padre* 'no father' is in Spec of TP. From the outer position the direct object can reconstruct to Spec of ClP and this accounts for the necessary agreement between the clitic and the direct object.

As for the differences between pre-verbal and post-verbal subjects, for Zubizarreta (1998), the post-verbal subject in (72) remains in its VP-internal position, is focused, and does not violate the NSR, and the pre-verbal subject in (73) is in Spec of TP.

Differentiating between direct object fronting in OVS structures in Quechua and Spanish depends crucially on projecting ClP in Spanish but not in Quechua, given the analyses for fronted direct objects in Quechua proposed in the previous subsection and the one adopted for Spanish. OVS word order in Quechua involves movement of the direct object to Spec of TopP, while OVS in Spanish involves an object that is base-generated in Spec of ClP and agrees with the clitic. In both languages the verb moves but for different reasons. In Spanish, it moves to the head of ClP while in Quechua it moves to the head of Focus Phrase. What this entails for the bilingual grammar is that in cases of interference the possibility of movement versus base-generation of the direct object will be affected by the licensing properties of the head of ClP that allows a base-generated DP in its specifier position.

In the case of OSV, the fronted direct object is base-generated in the specifier of Topic Phrase in Quechua and the verb stays inside the VP. In Spanish the direct object moves to Spec of ClP and further up and the verb moves to Cl. This implies that in order to distinguish between the two different underlying representations for the same superficial word order in both languages it is crucial to project ClP in Spanish and to not include Cl as part of the numeration in Quechua.

2.3.3 Fronted verbs

Spanish VSO structures such as (74) have received similar analyses in the literature (Suñer 1994, Ordoñez 1998 and Zubizarreta 1998):

(74) (No) levantó Juan la mano antes de interrumpir
 (not) raised Juan the hand before interrupting
 'Juan (didn't) raise his hand before interrupting' (Suñer 1994, p. 353)

According to these analyses, V raises to the highest inflectional projection of the verb, leaving the subject in Spec of VP and the object as complement of VP (Suñer 1994). This structure does not involve the projection of ClP. In that respect, the structures in Quechua and Spanish differ only with respect to how high the landing position is for V but they do not differ with respect to the VP-internal position of the subject and the direct object. The analysis of VOS structures is more complex. There are competing hypotheses that account for it. Suñer (1994) proposed that post-verbal subjects are right-adjoined to VP. Ordoñez (1998) challenges this analysis and proposes the Scrambling Hypothesis, according to which the object raises to the specifier of a functional category that dominates VP. He presents evidence from quantifier binding, Principle C effects and reconstruction effects that support the view that the object scrambles out of the VP in the overt syntax. Zubizarreta (1998) notices that, in VOS structures, the subject has narrow focus and bears nuclear stress and may be indefinite, precluding an analysis of scrambling motivated by definiteness as proposed by Diesing for German (1992):

(75) No trajo nada {Juan}.
 not brought anything
 'Juan did not bring anything' (Zubizarreta 1998, p. 126)

On the basis of these characteristics, Zubizarreta hypothesizes that VOS is derived from VSO and that the motivation for movement is to have the subject in a position in which it is assigned nuclear stress by the NSR. In her formulation of p-movement, she builds in the notion that it only affects nodes that have contradictory prosodic properties (i.e. if they are metrical sister nodes and one is assigned prominence by the NSR and the other by the FPR). Thus, she derives VOS from leftward adjunction of the lower VP to the higher VP. Once that movement has applied, the NSR and the FPR can apply and not yield a contradictory output. Unfortunately, research on the intonational patterns of Quechua is scarce and there is *a priori* no evidence in favor of a similar analysis for VOS in Quechua that is motivated by the same reasons.[20] If Zubizarreta's analysis for Spanish is correct, then VOS word order in Quechua and in Spanish differ crucially in that it involves verb movement and object scrambling in Quechua and leftward adjunction of lower VP in Quechua. Due to the initial stages of research on the intonational patterns of Quechua, it will be very difficult to make predictions about interference or convergence in this case that are solely based on functional features.

2.3.4 Clitic and clitic doubling structures as related to Topic or Focus

Finally, in order to further understand how interference and convergence may take place in the grammars of Quechua-Spanish bilinguals, it is necessary to examine the different clitic-related structures that are possible in Spanish and how they interact with antecedents in discourse. Especially since these syntactic structures may be interpreted differently depending on the discourse conditions in which they are uttered. There are two clitic-related structures that are topic-related structures. These are the clitic and the clitic doubling structures represented in (77), (78) and (79), contrasting with a direct object without a clitic in (76).

(76) Vi a Juan$_i$.
 saw to Juan$_i$
 'I saw Juan'

(77) Lo$_i$ saludé.
 Cl$_i$ greeted
 'I greeted him'

---

20. See O'Rourke (2003) for initial work on the peak alignment and the intonational patterns of Spanish in contact with Quechua.

(78) Lo$_i$ saludé a Juan$_i$.
      Cl$_i$ greeted to Juan$_i$
      'I greeted Juan'

(79) Lo$_i$ vi   a él$_i$.
      Cl$_i$ greeted to him$_i$
      'I greeted HIM'

In several varieties of Spanish (77) and (79) are grammatical, but (78) is not. In many Latin American varieties of Spanish including most Peruvian varieties, (77), (78) and (79) are possible. In fact, in some varieties of Andean Spanish spoken in Peru in language contact situations, doubling is possible even with indefinites and without the characteristic preposition *a* as in (80), as noted by Luján (1987):

(80) Lo vi un libro/una   ventana.
      Cl saw a   book/a-FEM window
      'I saw a book/a window'

The pervasiveness of clitic doubling in Latin American Spanish has led some researchers to posit that clitics in Spanish are morphological agreement markers rather than actual pronouns (Suñer 1988, Franco 1993, Everett 1996). As pointed out by Suñer (1988), clitics in Spanish can be marked for specificity features. In her view, clitics in clitic-doubling varieties of Southern Cone Spanish are subject to a Matching Principle that requires matching of the clitic features and those of the doubled element. If one assumes this principle, then one must account for varieties allowing for (78) as not being subject to the matching principle. In fact, Everett (1996) proposes that clitics are the phonological spell-out of AgrO and different languages may impose parametric restrictions on the conditions under which such features are spelled out.

In this subsection, I will assume the view that in Peruvian Spanish varieties that allow sentences such as (80), clitics are clearly agreement morphemes. Such varieties do not require an exact matching of features. Presumably, in those varieties the clitic *lo* is not marked for specificity or gender and number features.

For those varieties that require matching and allow (77), (78) and (79), I will assume Sportiche's (1992) proposal that clitics move along with the verb to the head of ClP, and identify the abstract operator in CL, agreeing in features with the DP in the specifier position. This DP may be an abstract operator as in CLLD structures, a null Topic operator that binds a null pronoun in the object position in the case of the simple clitic or one that binds the overt DP *in situ* in the case of clitic doubling of a DP.

Given these assumptions, I would like to address the issue of how these competing structures interact with the topic/focus structure of the sentence. Doubling in (79) is required with a strong pronoun, even in non clitic doubling varieties of Spanish. It has a clearly emphatic or focused interpretation. This interpretation is compatible with a structure in which the doubled strong pronoun is marked for a [+Focus] feature that forces either a contrastive or a focused interpretation. Checking of that feature takes place at LF between the clitic in the ClP head and the doubled pronoun.

Clitic structures and clitic doubling structures that do not involve strong pronouns do not involve focus features. On the contrary, they interact with the interpretation of Topics in discourse. I would like to propose that the direct object clitic and the subject agreement marker in (77) refer back to two topics previously introduced in discourse. Thus they are old information. Notice that in many clitic doubling varieties of Spanish, (77) is a perfect continuation of (76) in discourse, but (78) is not. This leaves open the question of when (78) is possible in discourse. I would like to propose that (78) is possible as a sentence uttered at the beginning of a discourse that presupposes *Juan* as a topic or that reintroduces *Juan* as a potential topic in discourse. The latter case is exemplified in the following fragment:[21]

(81) Ayer   vi   a Beatriz.
     yesterday saw to Beatriz
     '(I) saw Beatriz yesterday'

(82) La saludé.
     Cl greeted
     '(I) greeted her'

(83) Después, vi   a Yesica, Mercedes y   Lucía que se acercaban.
     after   saw to Yesica Mercedes and Lucía that Cl approached
     'Then, I saw Yesica, Mercedes and Lucía approaching me'.

(84) La llevé a Beatriz a un lado para hablarle en privado.
     Cl took   Beatriz aside   to   talk-Cl in private
     'I took Beatriz aside to talk to her in private'.

In (84), the clitic doubling structure reinstates Beatriz as a topic in discourse.

To summarize, I have adopted the view that clitic doubling of overt

---

21. This fragment is based on data from monolingual children in the pilot study reported in Sanchez (2002).

pronouns involves checking of focus features while clitic structures and clitic doubling of overt DPs interact in discourse with the sentential topics. Clitic constructions are required if no other potential topics have been introduced in discourse and clitic doubling structures are required to reinstate a previously introduced topic. These characteristics will be of importance when assessing the role that focus and topic features have in providing the bilingual speaker with cues for the feature specification of the clitic that is associated with the head of ClP. In particular they will be of importance in analyzing the distribution of clitic structures in Spanish according to discourse antecedents in the oral production of Quechua-Spanish bilinguals.

2.3.5 Null objects

Finally, as has been previously noted in the literature (Campos 1988), most varieties of Spanish allow for generic null objects as illustrated in (85–86).

(85) ¿Compraste pan?
 bought bread
 'Did (you) buy bread?'

(86) Sí, compré e.
 yes bought *e*
 'Yes, I bought (some)'

As sequence (87) and (88) show, specific null objects are disallowed:

(87) ¿Compr-aste el pastel?
 buy-2PAST the cake
 'Did you buy the cake?'

(88) *Sí, compré e.
 yes bought *e*
 'Yes, (I) bought (it)' (Camacho, Sanchez and Paredes 1997, p. 57)

In situations in which Spanish is or has been in contact with languages that allow null definite objects, such as Spanish in contact with Basque (Landa 1995), Quechua[22] or Guaraní, some varieties have evolved that allow for such null objects, as illustrated by the following examples from Sanchez (1998):

---

22. Such a variety is Quiteño Spanish analyzed by Suñer and Yepez (1988). For analysis on null objects in Spanish in contact with Quechua, see Camacho, Paredes and Sanchez (1997), Sanchez (1998) and Sanchez (1999).

(89) (A) La Cenicienta en la vicharra le echó   [un plato de
        (to) the Cinderella in the kitchen Cl throw-3SG-PAST a dish of
        arroz]$_i$ en la ceniza e   la   Cenicienta recogía pro $_i$ llorando.
        rice   in the cinders and the Cinderella picked pro up crying
        '(And) in the kitchen she threw Cinderella a plate with rice in the cinders
        and Cinderella picked it up crying'

I will assume Sanchez's (1999)[23] proposal for Andean Spanish that null pronouns are headed by a null determiner. This determiner can be specified for ±definite and ±specific features. In monolingual Spanish, the null D in object position must be [−specific, −definite]. As proposed in Sanchez (1999), in contact situations, there is transfer of the full set of possibilities for D from Quechua to Spanish. A less restricted distribution of null objects found in bilingual Spanish or a more restricted distribution found in bilingual Quechua would be evidence in favor of the Functional Convergence Hypothesis because this would show a case in which constant activation of the features associated with D has resulted in the fusion of the functional features in the two languages.

To summarize, in this subsection, based on previous analyses of Spanish, I have presented the following syntactic properties of Spanish:

1. The canonical SVO word order involves subject raising to Spec of ClP and verb movement to Cl.
2. In OVS structures, O is base generated in SpecClP and the verb moves to Cl. The post-verbal subject remains in its VP-internal position.
3. In OSV structures, O moves from Spec ClP to a higher position and the verb moves to T. The pre-verbal subject is in SpecTP.
4. VSO involves raising of the verb to T.
5. VOS involves leftward adjuntion of VP to the higher vP.
6. Clitics are topic-related.
7. Clitic doubling is restricted to contexts in which the doubled object reinstates a topic.
8. Null pronouns are generic.
9. Strong pronouns are focused.

Properties 1–4 indicate that in Spanish verb movement is triggered by features associated with Cl or T but not with focus or evidentiality. This is a crucial

---

23. See Raposo (1998) for a similar proposal for European Portuguese and Uriagereka (1995) for the idea that clitics can be treated as bundles of features that may be inserted under D.

difference in the properties of verb movement in Quechua discussed previously. Property 5 involves movement of a constituent containing VO triggered by prosodic reasons. Properties 6–8 relate clitic constructions to topics in discourse and null pronouns to generic interpretations. This is also a sharp difference between the Spanish and the Quechua grammars since Quechua lacks clitics and null objects can have definite antecedents in Quechua. Property 9 is similar in the two languages.

2.3.6 Contrasting the two direct object systems

In this chapter, I have proposed that there are some syntactic and morphological representations that bilinguals must maintain as separate, if there is no interference in the morphosyntactic representations of their direct object systems in Quechua and Spanish. These are shown in Tables 7 and 8.

If, on the other hand, there is interference between the two systems, then the Functional Interference Hypothesis predicts interference in the features associated with functional categories that result in significant changes in the syntax. Additionally, the Functional Convergence Hypothesis states that fusion of

Table 7. Differences at the sentential level

Quechua	Spanish
No ClP projected.	ClP projected.
No verb movement in SOV.	Verb movement in SVO.
OVS: Object movement to SpecTop and verb movement to Focus.	OVS: Object base-generated in SpecClP and verb movement to Cl.
OSV: Object base generated in SpecTop and no verb movement.	OSV: Object movement to and beyond SpecClP and verb movement to Cl.
VSO: verb movement to Focus.	VSO: verb movement to T.
VOS: verb movement and object scrambling to SpecTP.	VOS: VP leftward adjoined to vP
No direct object agreement on third person. Only person agreement in other persons.	Direct object clitics involve definiteness, gender and number.
Agreement marking does not have a function related to the Focus/Topic structure of the sentence.	Clitic doubling structures with strong pronouns are focused. Clitic and clitic doubling structures are topic-related.
Clausal complements are nominalizations and unmarked for independent tense.	Clausal complements have a main tense (Full CPs).

Table 8. Differences at the DP-level

Quechua	Spanish
Null determiners.	Overt determiners (license null nouns).
Overt accusative case (licenses null nouns).	No overt accusative case (exception: Preposition *a*).
Definite null pronouns are topic-related.	Generic null pronouns are not topic-related.

functional features or convergence in a single set of functional features for equivalent categories in the two grammars takes place in the bilingual mind due to constant activation of those features. In the last section of this chapter, I will discuss previous studies on the acquisition of direct objects and pronominal systems.

2.4 Studies on direct objects, pronominal systems and word order in L1, L2 and bilingual situations involving Quechua and/or Spanish

The literature on the first, second language and bilingual acquisition of direct object systems has addressed different issues depending on the functional categories associated with direct object DPs and to overt and null pronouns. I will assume a view in which the direct object system involves all the phonologically overt DPs and null objects that are the internal argument or direct complement of a transitive verb.[24] In this subsection, I will provide an overview of different L1, L2 and Bilingual acquisition studies that have analyzed the process of acquisition of one or more of these structures in Spanish or Quechua under unified or independent analyses. Their findings will be briefly analyzed in order to have a clearer idea of which feature specifications are acquired late in monolingual acquisition, those which are unstable or are subject to transfer from Quechua into Spanish, and those which are affected in other L2/Bilingual Spanish varieties.

---

24. I assume that the direct object system includes all overt DPs *in situ* or in a fronted position as well as clitic structures, clitic doubling structures and clitic left dislocation structures.

2.4.1 Direct objects in first language acquisition

2.4.1.1 *Direct objects in Quechua first language acquisition*

Courtney (1998) conducted a study on first language acquisition by Quechua-speaking children in the region of Chalhuanca, Arequipa in the Southern Andes of Peru. Although in this book I will focus on two varieties that differ from the one studied by Courtney, her findings are relevant to the discussion of word order and accusative marking in the bilingual varieties. Courtney studied the naturalistic production of six Quechua-speaking children between the ages of 2;0 and 3;9 years. The children had very limited exposure to Spanish, and Quechua was clearly their first language.[25] Her work focused on the description of their syntactic development in areas such as: case and object marking, the representation of arguments and word order, reduplication, ellipsis, evidential focus, coordination, and subordination. Since there are no comparable studies of first language acquisition for the Quechua varieties that I analyze, I will concentrate on her results on case and object marking and word order, as they may serve as a source of comparison with my own findings.

With respect to internal arguments, direct objects in particular, Courtney found that at the earliest age range (2;5 to 2;6) the child participant JN produced direct objects with accusative marking but had some omissions. The following is an example of an omitted (required) accusative marker:

(90) Tata-y ata-yku-sha-n pelota-Ø.
dad-1POSS.SG kick-AUG-PROG-3SG ball-(ACC)
'My daddy is kicking the ball.'

Courtney notes that omissions in her data involve Spanish loan words, diminutives and demonstrative forms but are not systematic and are clearly outnumbered by correct forms. She considers them performance errors. Additionally, she notes that JN has some confusion between accusative and locative markers. This is understandable as accusative can mark some locative expressions. JN also overgeneralizes accusative marking to dative[26] and benefactive cases at

---

25. The children studied by Courtney lived in a language contact situation in which both Quechua and Spanish were spoken. However, in the sociolinguistic situation described by Courtney, Quechua is the language used more frequently at home and it is only through schooling that the children in Chalhuanca became exposed to Spanish. Therefore she considers the subjects in their study as undergoing a process of first language acquisition in Quechua.

26. Clahsen (1984) cited by Meisel (1986) noted similar facts for German monolingual acquisition. See Chapter 2 to for Van de Kerke's account of accusative overgeneralization in

age 2;6. Object verbal morphology involving first, second and third person transitions from direct to indirect object is acquired long after case marking, at around age 2;10. Before acquisition of direct object morphology, JN produces instances of first person direct object pronouns predominantly case-marked in accusative. This trait was also found in the speech of participant BT (2;10 to 3;1) but not in the data from FE (3;2 to 3;5). According to Courtney: "BT also appears to avoid case-marking multisyllabic nouns borrowed from Spanish" (Courtney 1998, p. 120). In general, Courtney considers the omissions of accusative marking to be very low in frequency and restricted to Spanish loan words, diminutives and demonstratives.

With respect to word order, she found that her youngest participant JN at ages 2;5 to 2;6 years had explicit subjects (85% of the total corpus of 137 utterances with two canonical elements). This percentage declined later at ages 2;7 and 2;8 when the subject verbal morphology became productive. She also found that 34% of her utterances were subject final, a marked word order in Quechua, while the adults in her study produced only 10% of subject final utterances. Her data for JN and two other participants show a gradual decline in subject final clauses and an increase in verb final clauses corresponding to the canonical word order of Quechua. She also found bare stems with no subject agreement morphemes. The following example from BJ (ages 2;10 to 3;1) exemplifies these phenomena:

(91) Carru-ta muna noqa.
 car-ACC want I
 'I want the car.'

Her participants produced all six possible orderings of subject, verb and complement. She also found a decline of explicit personal pronouns that coincided with the stage at which subject morphology was acquired.

Unfortunately, Courtney does not comment on null objects, although her data from JN at age 2;6 show early examples of null objects:

(92) Señorita qan [e] apa-y.
 señorita you e take-IMPERATIVE
 'Take (it) to the señorita.'

Four conclusions can be extracted from her work that relate to case marking and word order:

Quechua presented above.

1. Accusative case marking is robust in Quechua first language acquisition except for Spanish loan words.
2. Accusative case marking is acquired prior to direct object verbal morphology.
3. Final subjects are frequent at early stages of acquisition.[27] There is no evidence of a preference for SVO word orders in early Quechua acquisition.[28]
4. For subject JN, subject agreement morphology preceded object agreement morphology.

Additionally, there are instances of third person null objects in the speech of JN.

Courtney interprets the availability of direct object scrambling and the fact that the children, particularly JN, assign accusative case very early as evidence in support of the view that the functional projection AgrO is active since the very early stages of acquisition.

2.4.1.2 *Direct objects in Spanish first language acquisition*

López-Ornat, Fernandez, Gallo and Mariscal (1994) present first language acquisition data from, María, a monolingual Spanish-speaking child from ages 1;07 to 3;11. The variety of Spanish spoken by María is Peninsular Spanish and differs from the varieties of Spanish in this study. Nevertheless, just as the Quechua L1 data, the data from López-Ornat establish some points of comparison between Quechua and Spanish L1 acquisition.

Unlike Quechua, Spanish lacks direct object accusative markings except for the distinctive use of the preposition *a* with animate direct objects. López-Ornat, Fernandez, Gallo and Mariscal (1994) data show two instances of a clear distinction between inanimate and animate direct objects with the preposition *a* at age 2;01 (file 331). Example (93) lacks the preposition but the answer in (94) has it:

Inanimate Object
(93) Ya. M'a   compao uno sapato.
yes Cl-DAT-3SG have bought one shoe
'Yes. (She) has bought me one shoe.'

---

27. Pierce (1992) notes similar facts for French L1 acquisition.

28. Courtney also found out that subordinate structures in the form of nominalizations such as the ones described by Lefebvre and Muysken (1989) are very infrequent in the children's data and appear to be acquired late.

Animate Direct Object
(94) P: ¿Dónde vas?
 where go
 'Where do (you) go?'
 Z: A bu(s)ca a mama.
 to look-for PREP mom
 'To look for mom.'

Lopez-Ornat (1990) has proposed that the acquisition of direct object clitics is achieved by age 3 in Spanish first language acquisition. However, by age 2;02 María's data show occasional cases of difficulties in gender assignment, as shown in (95):

(95) Quitámelo la toalla. (M 2;02)
 take-Cl.DAT-Cl.MASC-ACC the towelFEM
 'Take the towel away from me.'

Some instances of clitic doubling with non-personal direct objects (supposedly not allowed in the adult grammar of monolingual Peninsular Spanish-speakers) can also be found in Maria's data around age 2;02 in imperative contexts. However, they do not seem to be frequent or form a pattern:[29]

(96) Sácamelo este cacharro.
 take-Cl-DAT-1SG-Cl-ACC-3SG this thing
 'Take this thing out for me.' (M 2;02)

(97) Quíta-lo$_i$ eto$_i$ (M 2;02).
 take-Cl-ACC-3SG$_i$ this$_i$
 'Take this away.'

Thus, monolingual acquisition of Peninsular Spanish apparently shows some occasional instability in early clitic acquisition.[30,31]

With respect to subjects and word order, Maria's data show the early presence of subject drop and subject agreement morphology; her first inflected verbal form (Gallo 1994) appears at age 1;09 in file 146:

---

29. Torrens and Wexler (1997) analyzed Maria's data and argue that she has an almost adult-like grammar with respect to Peninsular clitic doubling in her files ranging from age 1;7 to 3;11.
30. I will be very cautious about this evidence as it is only occasional.
31. See Schaeffer (2000) for a study on L1 acquisition of clitics in Italian and direct object scrambling in Dutch related to specificity and the acquisition of pragmatics.

(98) M: Ah Sento.
    ah (I) sit-1SG
    'I sit.'

From age 2;01, personal pronouns are incorporated as in the adult grammar:

(99) Poque   no. Ya   palitos, yo cojo   los gapalitos míos.
    because not already sticks   I   pick up the ga-sticks mine
    'Because. I pick up my sticks.'

Variations in the canonical SVO word order are frequent in María's speech and associated with clitic doubling or clitic left dislocation structures.

The work of Fujino and Sano (2000) presents evidence of null objects in Maria's data as well as in the data from two other Spanish-speaking children. Their analysis of spontaneous data shows that the acquisition of clitic pronouns coincides with a decrease in null object production alongside a constant rate of lexical noun phrase production. They argue that null objects in early child Spanish are empty categories substituting for clitics. The following are examples from Maria's speech at age 2;3:

(100) Hay que pompar [e] encima de la   silla.
    have that put   [e] on top of the chair
    '(We) have to put (it) on the chair.'

Thus, María's data shows evidence of:

1. An initial distinction between animate and inanimate direct objects evidenced by the use of the preposition *a* with animate direct objects.
2. Some instability in the acquisition of gender features for clitics.
3. Some deviant forms of clitic doubling regarding the features of the doubled element.
4. Other possible word orders in addition to the canonical SVO word order, particularly those associated with clitic left dislocated and clitic doubling structures.
5. Precedence in the acquisition of subject agreement morphology over clitics.
6. Early null objects.

To summarize, Quechua first language acquisition data show robust accusative marking from the early stages of acquisition. Instability in accusative marking appears to be due to overgeneralization and to the absence of marking on Spanish loan words. Spanish first language acquisition data show some evidence of early differentiation between inanimate and animate direct objects using the preposition *a*, but they show also some evidence of instability in the feature specification of clitics. Quechua and Spanish data show clear evidence that subject agreement morphology precedes object agreement morphology in first language acquisition. Despite being canonical SOV and SVO languages, Quechua and Spanish also show evidence of flexibility in word order. Quechua has some instances of null objects in early acquisition, and Spanish has non-adult-like null direct objects.

2.4.2 Direct objects in second language acquisition[32]

2.4.2.1 Direct objects in Spanish as a second language

There are several studies on the acquisition of direct objects in the L2 Spanish of Quechua speakers. In one of the pioneering works on Spanish dialectology in Peru, Escobar (1978) provided a general description of some of the characteristics of Spanish in contact with Quechua in the Andean regions of Peru.[33] He noticed that Andean Spanish in its bilingual variants was characterized by fronted objects in positions disallowed them in Peruvian Spanish Standard as exemplified in (101):

(101) A mi primo encontré en la fiesta.
       to my cousin found   in the party
       '(I) found my cousin at the party.' (Escobar, A. 1978, p. 109)

Escobar also noticed cases of gender and number mismatches in the feature specification of clitics:

(102) A mi hija   todos lo   adoramos.[34]
       to my daughter we all Cl-ACC-MASC-3SG adore
       'We all adore my daughter.' (Escobar, A. 1978, p. 110)

(103) No lo   vi a sus hermanitos.
       not Cl-ACC-3SG see to his siblings
       'I did not see his siblings.' (Escobar, A. 1978, p. 111)

---

32. To the best of my knowledge there are no studies on the acquisition of direct objects in Quechua as a second language, so I will present results of studies on the L2 acquisition of Spanish direct objects.

33. Other works that have analyzed L2 Spanish word order are: Lozano (1975), Cerrón-Palomino (1976) and Luján and Minaya (1984)

34. This example is a case of clitic left dislocation.

Also instances of null definite articles in direct object position:

(104) María escribe carta.
 Maria writes letter
 'Maria writes (the) letter.' (Escobar, A. 1978, p. 108)

Later work by Escobar, A. M. (1994a) among Quechua-Spanish bilinguals noted instances of null objects with definite and specific antecedents as in:[35]

(105) A veces   en la noche dejo   su   quacker ya   preparado, en la
 sometimes in the night (I) leave their quacker already prepared in the
 mañana   [e] calientan y [e] toman.
 morning (they) [e] heat   and [e] eat
 'Sometimes at night (I) leave their quacker already prepared, in the morning they heat (it) and eat (it)' (Escobar, A. M. 1994a., p. 89)

In the field of generative SLA, previous studies on the L2 Spanish direct objects of Quechua speakers have focused on the analysis of transfer of the feature specifications of AgrO from Quechua to L2 Spanish. Camacho, Paredes and Sánchez (1997) propose that, at least at the initial stages of acquisition, there is transfer of the Quechua pronominal value for null objects to Spanish, as illustrated by the following example from their low proficiency group data.

(106) a. ¿Mata (el lobo) a la oveja$_i$?
   kill (the wolf) to the sheep?
   'Does (the wolf) kill the sheep?'
 b. Mata [e$_i$].
   kills [e$_i$]
   'Yes, (it) kills (it).' (Camacho, Paredes, Sanchez 1997, p. 57)

This view of pervasive transfer of the null object values has also been explored in Sanchez's (1998) study of L1 and L2 speakers of Spanish in the area of Ulcumayo. In that study, I presented data from older children and adolescents (ages 10–17)

---

35. In a study on the L2 acquisition of Spanish by speakers of French, English, German, Chinese, Japanese and Korean speakers, Liceras and Díaz (1999) found no conclusive evidence of null objects. This is particularly puzzling in the case of Chinese, Japanese and Korean speakers because their L1 has them. They did find frequent cases of clitic doubling. Perhaps their subjects were in the process of overgeneralizing clitics as agreement markers and as such they were incompatible with null objects.

attending a secondary school in the town of Ulcumayo.[36] At a descriptive level, the data showed approximately equal frequencies of overt objects and clitics in the narratives told by the children and adolescents but a higher frequency of null objects among native speakers of Spanish. Their null objects had definite and/or specific antecedents, as shown by the following example:

(107) ¿Qué cosa es **esta cajita**$_i$? Para no abrir [e$_i$] le ha dicho.
what thing is this box$_i$ not to-open [e$_i$] Cl-DAT-3SG has said
'What is this box? In order not to open (it), he said'

In that work, I concluded that even the L1 variety had reset its parametric values to include null objects with definite and specific antecedents.

With respect to word order variation, Muysken (1984) provides evidence of OV word orders in the L2 Spanish of Quechua speakers. He finds no evidence of SOV word orders but some evidence of OV word orders. He proposes that OV word orders are the result of preposing the object to a clause initial position, as part of stylistic movement available in all varieties of Spanish.[37]

Camacho (1999) accounts for word order differences between L2 Spanish of Quechua speakers and monolingual Spanish by distinguishing between parametric values that can be reset and those that cannot be successfully reset because of target evidence that is compatible with the setting of the first language. In his study, Camacho argues that the Spanish interlanguage of Quechua speakers is characterized by transfer of two independent parameters: the possibility of licensing null objects with definite/specific antecedents (cf., Camacho, Paredes and Sanchez 1997), and a feature triggering object movement for sentential focus that yields SOV word order. Spanish does allow for topicalization, that is, the fronting of direct objects in main clauses, as long as they are generic. Contreras (1976) has proposed that these generic fronted objects are doubled by a null clitic in the sentence:

(108) Luces naturales, no sé si tengo.
lights natural not know if have
'(I) don't know if (I) have natural lights' (Contreras 1976, p. 85)

---

36. Unlike the children in the study reported in this book, the children whose data was analyzed in Sanchez (1998) came from a wider variety of towns although they all attended school in Ulcumayo.

37. Muysken uses the general term X, to refer to objects and prepositional phrases.

Nevertheless, Spanish disallows such structures in infinitival clauses, irrespectively of whether they have a resumptive pronoun or not:

(109) *Iré para maíz$_i$ comprar (lo$_i$).
 go for corn$_i$ to buy (it$_i$)
 '(I) will go in order to buy corn'

The data from adult learners in early stages of acquisition supports the view that L2 Spanish speakers allow for fronted objects that are licensed by a null object pronoun in contexts in which they are ruled out in the target language:

(110) a. ¿Y tú vuelves a Ayacucho para ayudar a tus padres en la chacra?
 'Do you return to Ayacucho to help your parents on the farm?'
 b. Sí claro, maíz (...) para cultivarlo, para sembrar [e]
 yes sure corn to plant to sow [e]
 'Yes, sure, to plant corn.' (Camacho 1999, p. 124)

In a pilot study conducted among Quechua-Spanish L2/Bilinguals prior to the study presented in this present study (Sanchez 2002), I found similarities in the distribution of direct object structures in the two languages. Strong pronouns were infrequent in the L2/Bilingual children's data. Pronominal null objects and topicalizations were slightly more frequent in the L2/Bilingual data than in the comparison monolingual data and CP complements were very infrequent in the L2/Bilingual data. Spanish structures such as clitic, clitic doubling and clitic left dislocation were found with similar frequencies in the L1 Spanish and the L2/bilingual data. However, in the L2/Bilingual data, null objects exhibited anaphoric and deictic properties, whereas in the L1 Spanish stories these properties do not appear to be clearly distinct. Clitic doubling was used in L2/Bilingual Spanish to maintain the same topic in the discourse but not in L1 Spanish. In the analysis of the pilot data, I related those differences to discourse conditions on the topic structure of the sentence. In this book, I will continue to explore that line of analysis.

To summarize, studies on the L2 acquisition of Spanish direct objects by Quechua speakers have emphasized the pervasive nature of transfer of the feature specification of null objects from Quechua into Spanish, as well as the transfer of canonical word order that is compatible with evidence in the target language.[38] These studies have also shown that some properties such as strong

---

38. On the other hand, Kalt (2001) studied the acquisition of reflexive and oblique clitics in the L2 Spanish of Quechua speakers from Bolivia and did not find evidence of transfer of the

pronouns do not appear to be transferred and that clitics are acquired by L2/bilinguals but may have different discourse properties.

2.4.3 Direct objects in bilingual language acquisition

Research on Basque-Spanish bilingual children could shed some light on the study of Quechua-Spanish bilingualism. The work of Ezeizabarrena (1997) on the L1 acquisition of subject and object morphology in two bilingual children in the Basque country shows data with two of the same characteristics studied here. Her data show a progression in which subject morphology is acquired before object morphology and the data are characterized by null objects. Mikel (M) and Jurgi (J), the children in her study, had productive subject agreement morphology at ages 1;11 and and 2;06 respectively. On the other hand, direct object clitics did not become productive in Mikel's speech until the age of 2;01 and in Jurgi until 3;05. The following are examples that show this production:

(111) He/ha (M 1;11)
 '(I) have/(s/he) has'

(112) Voy/vamos (M 1;11)
 '(I) go, (we) go'

(113) Cogo (=cojo) (J 2;06)
 'I catch'

(114) Qu(i)ero (J 2;06)
 '(I) want'

(115) Y ahora esto lo tengo que poner. (M 3;04)
 and now this Cl-MASC-3SG have that put
 'And now (I) have to put this'

Also, like Quechua and Bilingual varieties of Spanish in contact with Quechua, Basque Spanish is characterized by null clitics in the third person. Ezizebarrena observed few "errors" in clitic placement in her subjects; however, she observed a defective use of singular forms for plural ones (the masculine singular clitic *lo* used instead of the plural masculine form *los*). She also observed "errors" in the use of gender in third person object clitic such as the use of the feminine clitic *la* for the masculine clitic *lo* that could be attributed to interference from Basque.

The studies discussed in this section provide an overview of first, second

---

L1 functional features into the L2.

language and early bilingual acquisition of the direct object systems in Quechua and Spanish. The study on Quechua first language acquisition favors the continuity approach and the notion of an early presence of the functional categories Agreement Object (AgrO^0) and Determiner (D^0). It also shows the robustness of accusative case marking in early child language with the notable exception of Spanish loan words. The data from Spanish first language acquisition also show evidence of an early distinction between animate and inanimate objects. Both Spanish and Quechua acquisition data indicate that subject agreement emerges before object agreement. Nevertheless, there is some evidence of instability in the development of Spanish clitics with respect to features such as gender and number.

Second language acquisition studies of Spanish have shown evidence of transfer of the L1 feature values for AgrO^0 at early stages of L2 acquisition. Studies conducted at early stages of acquisition among children bilingual in Spanish and languages other than Quechua also show evidence of cross-linguistic interference in this respect. Thus, most of the evidence presented in this sub-section point in the direction of cross-linguistic interference in direct objects and direct object agreement. If one assumes that functional categories are present from the early stages of acquisition and that interference may also take place from early stages, the question that arises is whether interference continues until the children reach the steady state. In this study, I will propose that the functional features of categories such as determiners and clitics associated with the direct object pronominal system are ideal candidates for a continuous cross-linguistic influence that, at the steady state, becomes convergence in the specification of functional features.

CHAPTER 3

Bilinguals in a language contact situation

In order to find an appropriate group of individuals to participate in research conducted on linguistic interference and convergence in functional categories, I located populations whose speech showed evidence of interference in social situations where language contact had been pervasive among individuals over at least two generations and among which constant activation of the two languages was the norm. This task was made difficult because language shift tends to take place in the short period between two generations. Furthermore, it was necessary to identify bilingual children whose parents or guardians were bilinguals themselves in order to control for exposure to input in the two languages at home.

3.1 The language contact and language shift situations

An ideal language contact situation was found among Quechua-Spanish bilinguals. At the higher clausal level, the two languages differ significantly, especially with respect to verb movement as related to different functional projections, as shown in Chapter 2, and also with respect to the feature specification for overt and null object pronouns. Thus, they are the ideal testing ground for convergence in specific sets of functional features. These populations are also ideal because Quechua and Spanish have been in contact in different geographical areas of Peru since colonial times. The degrees and frequency of contact have changed and evolved throughout history; despite prolonged contact, some areas of Peru have exhibited a pattern of language shift that has favored monolingualism in Spanish.

One of the main factors affecting the rate at which the language shift processes take place is whether the environment is rural or urban. Language shift in Peru has followed a pattern similar to that analyzed by Gal (1979) in which the urban/rural distinction plays a very important role. In the Quechua-speaking rural areas of the country, the shift of dominance from Quechua into

Spanish among bilingual communities may be accelerated by the return of migrants from urban areas, by the establishment of new roads and communication media, and by better Spanish monolingual education programs; but even when Quechua is stigmatized, the shift tends to be slower in rural areas than in cities.[1] In large urban zones such as the capital Lima, a Spanish-dominant environment, language shift usually takes place among migrant communities from Quechua-speaking rural areas. For these communities language shift has been rapid and accomplished in one generation. Evidence for this shift from Quechua to Spanish among migrant communities to the city of Lima has been analyzed since the 1970's. Myers (1973) shows that Quechua-Spanish bilingual migrants from rural areas who settle in the city of Lima usually exhibit a pattern of strong preference for Spanish, particularly with their children, and tend to accelerate the pattern of language shift.[2]

These different patterns of language shift have created a situation in which Quechua-Spanish bilingual speakers in rural areas and monolingual speakers of Spanish can be located on opposite sides of a sociolinguistic continuum (Escobar 1978) in the contact situation. In this study, I present and analyze data that characterize this type of language contact situation: the "monolinguals" in urban settings and the "bilinguals" in rural settings are not necessarily two discrete and separate sociolinguistic communities but rather part of a linguistic continuum. In that context, I will use the term "monolingual" to refer to speakers who may have been exposed to another language but whose knowledge and use of that language is limited to passive knowledge of isolated words.

---

1. Zuñiga (1987) is against assuming a generalized Quechua-Spanish bilingualism for rural areas of the Southern Andes of Peru. In fact, in many rural areas of the country the shift is more apparent than real as many speakers with low levels of proficiency in Spanish describe themselves as bilinguals due to the higher prestige of Spanish and as a strategy to overcome the discrimination suffered by Quechua speakers.

2. The situation Myers (1973) describes is very complex and the issue of language shift is also related to factors such as the domain or the location of the conversation, the type of situation (formal vs. informal) or, in speaking with relatives, the sex (slightly more Spanish is spoken with male relatives than with female relatives). Myers shows evidence that more Spanish is used with younger relatives than with relatives the same age or older. Out of 140 participants, 86.4% responded that they always spoke in Spanish with their younger male relatives in a formal situation and 91% in an informal situation and up to 67% in an intimate situation. For younger female relatives the percentages were 85.6% in a formal situation, 89.9% in an informal situation and 65.2% in an intimate situation.

The bilingual groups studied are second-generation bilinguals living in a rural environment where language shift from Quechua to Spanish is taking place. The study of their knowledge of both languages allows for the exploration of the long-term consequences of language contact on the two languages spoken in a bilingual community. More precisely, it allows for the study of the syntactic representation of two languages in the minds of bilinguals who have received input in the two languages at home and in the community and who are used to the constant activation of the two languages. The study of interference and convergence among such bilinguals will shed some light on the issue of the predictability of interference and convergence in a context of language contact and language shift.

The "monolingual" children whose data are analyzed are children who may receive some exposure to Quechua but do not use the language themselves. These children live in a Spanish-speaking urban area in the city of Lima, and despite the fact that they may have at least one parent or caretaker who is bilingual in Quechua and Spanish and who may sometimes address them in Quechua, they do not consider themselves as bilinguals nor do they have proficiency in Quechua except for some very basic knowledge of isolated words or idiomatic expressions. In their environment, Quechua is highly stigmatized and not spoken in the public domain. I selected these children as the comparison group for the Spanish data from the bilingual children because, at the national level, the Spanish spoken by them has increasingly become the norm in society at large although it does not correspond to the variety of Spanish spoken by the elites. Whether these children have some passive knowledge of Quechua is a moot point, since it is clear that the majority of input these children receive is in Spanish and the frequency of Spanish input for these children is greater than for the bilingual children in the two groups that are the focus of my study. Due to the nature of the language contact population sought, no Quechua monolingual children living in the rural areas were found, and for that reason, I did not include such a comparison group.[3]

---

3. Quechua monolingual children could perhaps be identified in other rural areas of the country. However, as Quechua is not a standardized language with a wide use at the national level or in media communications, it would have been very difficult to identify a group of monolingual speakers whose speech may be taken by other Quechua speakers as an accepted standard.

3.2 The geographical areas of language contact

Language contact between Spanish and Quechua dates back to the beginning of colonization in the sixteenth century. Before then, Quechua was one of the main languages spoken in large areas of what constitutes Peru's territory today. In the pre-colonial era, Quechua expanded throughout the territory at different paces in different periods, and as a result, a range of dialectal varieties emerged. Parker (1963) and Torero (1964) propose a division between two Quechua families of dialects: the Quechua I or Quechua B family and the Quechua II or Quechua A family (Parker 1963, Torero 1964). The varieties that form the Quechua I/B linguistic family are presently spoken in the Central Andes of Peru. These are the dialects that Torero posits as the oldest varieties with a greater level of variation at the phonological level (Torero 1964). The dialects that belong to the Quechua II/A family are the varieties spoken in the Southern Andes of Peru and in some areas of the Amazonian region, as well as in Bolivia, Ecuador, Northern Argentina and Colombia (Cerrón-Palomino 1987).

For this study I selected a variety of Quechua from each of the two main families: Ulcumayo Quechua, part of the Quechua I family, and Lamas Quechua, spoken in the department of San Martin in the provinces of Sisa, Lamas and some areas of other provinces, and part of the Quechua II family. These two varieties differ with respect to their phonological systems, certain areas of the lexicon and a subset of suffixes. However, for the purpose of my study, they are ideal because they do not exhibit significant differences in terms of the syntax of direct object complements and they are in situations of prolonged contact that are rapidly evolving into a shift from Quechua to Spanish.

3.2.1 Bilingualism in the district of Ulcumayo

The district of Ulcumayo consists of a population of 9877 according to the 1993 Peru National Census data.[4] It comprises a central town called Ulcumayo and about 40 *caseríos* or small villages located in the mountains surrounding the main town. Its urban population in the 1993 census was 2,518, while its rural population was 7,359. Its growth rate between the 1981 and the 1993 census was −0.80. The rate of illiteracy among the population 15 years and older is 26%

---

4. This census is the most recent population census available from Peru's Instituto Nacional de Estadística e Informática.

and the percentage of the population 15 years and older who completed their elementary education (up to the sixth grade) is 47.7%.

In terms of its sociolinguistic composition, the community is bilingual. The 1993 census reported a total of 5,913 speakers of Spanish, 2,452 speakers of Quechua and 7 speakers of Aymara. Among the segment of the population between ages 5–14 the census reported a total of 2,347 speakers of Spanish and only 303 speakers of Quechua (a ratio of 7.74). However, as in many Quechua-speaking communities of the Central Andes, Quechua is a highly stigmatized language (Cerrón-Palomino 1989) and in some of the surrounding villages it is perceived as a disappearing language. As a consequence, the answer to the questions on language in the 1993 census questionnaire might have been biased. Despite this possible bias, the census provides a picture of the language shift that is taking place in the community. Table 1 shows the population divided according to the language acquired at an early age for each age range.

Table 1. Languages acquired at an early age by the population in the Ulcumayo district

Language learned at an early age	Total	Men	Women	5 to 14 yrs	15 to 24 yrs	25 to 34 yrs	35 to 44 yrs	45 to 54 yrs	55 to 64 yrs	65 and more yrs
Ulcumayo District	8475	4320	4155	2683	1864	1358	829	703	584	454
Spanish	5913	3155	2758	2347	1501	952	475	311	211	116
Quechua	2452	1117	1335	303	334	382	346	384	370	333
Aymara	7	2	5	–	3	–	2	2	–	–
Another native language	22	8	14	11	1	8	–	1	1	–
Foreign language	2	–	2	–	1	1	–	–	–	–
No answer	79	38	41	22	24	15	6	5	2	5

Peru National Census 1993
Source: Instituto Nacional de Estadística e Informática (INEI)

As Table 1 shows, the 1993 census indicates an increasing shift in the proportion of the population responding that Quechua was acquired at an early age. For the three cohorts above the age of 45, there are more early acquirers of Quechua than for the early cohorts. Although the census data do not necessarily present an exact description of the sociolinguistic situation, they reveal a tendency in language attitudes that may, in turn, reflect the type of language shift that is taking place in Ulcumayo.

In terms of education, there are no bilingual education programs in Quechua and Spanish in the district, only monolingual programs in Spanish.

However, the school does not necessarily accomplish the goals of total immersion in Spanish.

There is a high degree of mobility between the central town and the *caseríos* in the district that is encouraged by the fact that many children from the *caseríos* study in Ulcumayo. In the study, the team of research assistants and I interviewed children from three schools: the Mariategui elementary school and the Tupac Amaru school located in the central town of Ulcumayo, and the school 31249 in the *caserío* of Apán.[5]

3.2.2 Bilingualism in the district of Wayku, Lamas

The second group of bilingual children comes from a small village in the district of Lamas. The district has a population of 13,651, according to the 1993 census data. It includes nine *barrios* or neighborhoods. One of them, the Barrio Wayku, recently designated as the Centro Poblado Menor del Wayku, is where most of the Quechua-speaking population is concentrated. There are also Quechua-speaking populations in some surrounding areas and in other provinces in the department of San Martín (Pardo, Doherty and Sangama 2001). The participants interviewed for this study came mostly from the Wayku; however, statistical data from the 1993 census for the town of Wayku alone are not available. For this reason, I will present data for the whole district of Lamas, although these data include the monolingual (Spanish) main town of Lamas.

The urban population of the district in the 1993 census was 8,584 while its rural population was 5,067. Most of the Wayku population lives in a rural environment although with very close access to an urban environment (the town of Lamas). The growth rate of the district of Lamas between the 1981 and the 1993 census was 1.60. The percentage of the population 15 years and older is 60.39%. The rate of illiteracy among the population 15 years and older is 19.90% and the percentage of these that have completed their elementary education (sixth grade) was 61.2%.

In terms of its sociolinguistic composition, the district of Lamas has a bilingual community in the small town of Wayku and the surrounding fields. The Lamas Quechua-speaking community is peculiar since it is one of the few Quechua-speaking communities located in the Amazonian region. The central

---

5. In terms of their place of origin, 10 of the children interviewed for this study came from the town of Ulcumayo and 10 from the caserío of Apán. The other children were from the *caseríos* of Allpamina, Chaqchas, Libertad, Muriucru, Pucayacu, Huanuco and Quilcatacta.

town of Lamas has a population that is mostly monolingual in Spanish. Despite the isolated nature of the Lamas Quechua speaking community in the town of Wayku, there is an increase in positive linguistic attitudes among its leaders and in the community in general, as attested by their acceptance of a bilingual education program at the elementary levels. There is also a great degree of pride in their traditions among some members of the community. Despite language shift, a group of community leaders in Wayku take language as an index of cultural identity and consider bilingual education programs as a key to the development of the "Lamista Kechwa" communities (Pardo, Doherty and Sangama 2001). Indeed Wayku is perceived as the focal center of the Lamista culture that encompasses other Quechua-speaking communities in other provinces such Bellavista, El Dorado, Huallaga, Picota, San Martín and Mariscal Cáceres (Pardo, Doherty and Sangama 2001).

Table 2. Languages acquired at an early age by the population in the Lamas District

Language learned at an early age	Total	Men	Women	5 to 14 yrs	15 to 24 yrs	25 to 34 yrs	35 to 44 yrs	45 to 54 yrs	55 to 64 yrs	65 and more yrs
Lamas district	11886	5929	5957	3642	2421	1972	1394	1015	759	683
Spanish	10687	5409	5278	3413	2243	1754	1227	851	618	581
Quechua	1063	456	607	183	153	196	157	150	133	91
Aymara	5	3	2	1	2	2	–	–	–	–
Another native language	15	9	6	2	4	3	1	2	2	1
Foreign language	1	1	–	–	–	1	–	–	–	–
No answer	115	51	64	43	19	16	9	12	6	10

Peru IX National Census — 1993
Source: Instituto Nacional de Estadística e Informática (INEI).

The 1993 census reported a total of 10,687 speakers of Spanish and 1,063 speakers of Quechua in the district of Lamas. Once again it should be noted that the total of Spanish speakers includes both the Wayku population and the monolingual town of Lamas.

Among the population 5–14 the census reported 3,413 speakers of Spanish and 183 speakers of Quechua (a ratio of 18.6). Unlike the case of Ulcumayo, there is not a decrease in the absolute number of speakers across cohorts although proportionally to the number of Spanish speakers, the situation appears to show evidence of language shift. It may also reveal an increase in the monolingual Spanish-speaking population of the town of Lamas. Thus, although

Quechua is highly stigmatized by the Spanish-speaking community, the fact that the district of Wayku constitutes an island of Lamista-Quechua culture and tradition seems to concur with language maintenance efforts such as elementary bilingual education, a community effort not encountered in Ulcumayo.

3.2.3 "Monolingual" San Juan de Miraflores

San Juan de Miraflores is one the districts surrounding the city of Lima. Its creation and expansion are the result of the massive rural migration to the capital that took place in the 1950s. According to the 1993 Census, it has a population of 217,000 inhabitants, all of whom live in an urban area. Its growth rate between the1981 and the 1993 census was 3.30% per annum. In 1993, 69.20% of its population was 15 years old or older and their rate of illiteracy was 4.10%, significantly lower than in the rural districts of Ulcumayo and Lamas. The percentage of the population aged 15 and older who have completed their elementary education (sixth grade) is 87, also significantly higher than in the rural areas of Ulcumayo and Lamas.

The 1993 census reported a total of 210,609 speakers of Spanish and 36,763 speakers of Quechua in the district of San Juan de Miraflores. Among 5–14 years old speakers, the census reported 41,572 speakers of Spanish and 8693 speakers of Quechua (a ratio of 4.78, the lowest of the three groups). The district of San Juan de Miraflores is a community in which Spanish is dominant in the public domain and in many households, and Quechua is highly stigmatized. Of the three populations studied here, San Juan de Miraflores is the one in which Quechua is most stigmatized. The attitudes towards Quechua are

Table 3. Languages acquired at an early age by the population in the San Juan district

Language learned at an early age	Total	Men	Women	5 to 14 yrs	15 to 24 yrs	25 to 34 yrs	35 to 44 yrs	45 to 54 yrs
	252174	62840	62650	51460	34064	19006	12527	9627
Spanish	210609	60486	55279	41572	24846	12769	8766	6891
Quechua	36763	1787	6512	8693	8144	5595	3439	2593
Aymara	3453	131	593	911	924	540	253	101
Another native language	204	55	55	44	16	15	14	5
Foreign language	225	51	62	46	21	19	16	10
No answer	920	330	149	194	113	68	39	27

Peru IX National Census — 1993
Source: Instituto Nacional de Estadística e Informática (INEI).

negative among the children as evidenced by those manifested in the interviews. The teachers also showed a negative attitude towards all indigenous languages; this was demonstrated by their lack of desire to use them for academic purposes or to allow the students to use them in the classroom.

3.2.4 Bilingual and "monolingual" participants

The data collected in this book derive from the three groups of children ages 8–13 described in the previous section. The first group consists of 28 Quechua-Spanish bilingual children living in the district of Ulcumayo, province of Junín, department of Junín. They consider themselves bilingual in Quechua and Spanish and receive their education only in Spanish. The second group consists of 30 children from the town of Wayku in the district of Lamas, province of Lamas, department of San Martín. Like the children from Ulcumayo, they consider themselves bilinguals in Quechua and Spanish but receive education in Quechua and in Spanish. The third group was composed by 36 Spanish-speaking children from the San Juan de Miraflores district in the city of Lima. This latter group lives in a Spanish dominant community. Their knowledge of Quechua is limited to isolated words or idiomatic chunks and have at least one Quechua-Spanish bilingual parent. The number of children and their percentages in the sample are shown in Table 4.

Table 4. Place of origin

Place of origin	Number of children	
San Juan de Miraflores	36	(38.3%)
Lamas	30	(31.9%)
Ulcumayo	28	(29.8%)
Total	94	(100.0%)

I selected children in the age range 8–13 for two reasons: First, I wanted to report on bilingual children whose process of acquisition of the two languages had reached a steady state and was no longer undergoing significant changes. Second, due to the types of tests used in order to investigate the syntactic representation of the pronominal system in these children, I preferred children whose command of pictorial representations was high and, in rural areas of Peru, this is mostly accomplished between fourth and sixth grade. As a result of this selection, the children had been in school at least for three years, they had

Table 5. Children according to grade and age

Place of origin		4	5	6	All
San Juan de Miraflores	Average	8.6	10.1	11.2	9.9
	S. D.	0.768	0.793	0.603	1.282
	Max.	10	12	12	12
	Min	8	9	10	8
	Total of children	13	12	11	36
Lamas	Average	9.7	11.0	11.7	10.7
	S. D.	0.786	1.155	1.000	1.258
	Max.	11	13	13	13
	Min	9	9	11	9
	Total of children	11	10	9	30
Ulcumayo	Average	10.0	10.8	11.7	10.8
	S. D.	1.348	1.169	1.160	1.424
	Max.	13	12	13	13
	Min	9	9	10	9
	Total of children	12	6	10	28

been exposed to books, and would be able to recognize pictures. Some differences between the monolingual urban group and the two bilingual rural groups were found in terms of the average age. This difference is due to the fact that the children interviewed were selected from fourth to sixth grades and the age entering school is lower in the urban district than in the rural ones. Table 5 shows the children's average age according to grade, since there is a tendency for the urban children to enter school at a younger age, seven of the 4th graders in San Juan were eight years old, while all of the rural children were at least nine.

With respect to sex, I tried to keep a balance between the populations. In San Juan, out of a total of the 36 children, 18 were male and 18 were female. In Lamas out of the 30 children that participated, 14 were girls and 16 were boys. In Ulcumayo 17 girls and 11 boys took part in the study.

When asked for their mother tongue, all the children in San Juan claimed to be native speakers of Spanish. In Lamas and Ulcumayo the situation was different: 15 of the children in Lamas claimed Spanish as their mother tongue, 9 claimed Quechua and 6 claimed to be bilingual from birth. In Ulcumayo, 11 said Spanish was their mother tongue, 10 claimed Quechua and 7 self-identified as bilinguals form birth. These data are shown in Table 6 and reflect the perceptions of the Ulcumayo and Lamas groups.

Given the complex language contact situation in which these children live,

Table 6. Children according to declared L1

Place of origin	Spanish	Quechua	Quechua and Spanish	Total
San Juan de Miraflores	36 (100%)	0	0	36 (100%)
Lamas	15 (50%)	9 (30%)	6 (20%)	30 (100%)
Ulcumayo	11 (39.29%)	10 (35.71%)	7 (25%)	28 (100%)

their self-assessment was insufficient to classify them as having Quechua or Spanish as their native language. It was necessary to analyze their answers to the questions about the type and frequency of input they had received at home.

3.3 Patterns of linguistic input at home

In order to determine the frequency of input in the two languages received by the children at home, I asked them about their relatives' use of languages at home. The following tables show the results by relative, each one shows evidence of language shift. Table 7 shows a much higher rate of Spanish input from the mothers of the children in San Juan in comparison with those of the children in Lamas and Ulcumayo. Table 7 shows that 69.4% of the children in San Juan de Miraflores declared that their mothers spoke to them in Spanish only, while only 6.7% and 10.7% claimed the same in Lamas and Ulcumayo, respectively. Despite the fact that 25% of the children in San Juan asserted that their mothers spoke to them in both Quechua and Spanish, when probed about their language proficiency in Quechua the children were only able to use isolated words and phrases. The percentages of children who reported that their mothers spoke to them in both languages was higher for Lamas and Ulcumayo (73.3% and 53.6%, respectively).

Table 7. Language used by the mother to address the child

Place of origin	Spanish	Quechua	Quechua and Spanish	Children without a mother	Total
San Juan de Miraflores	25 (69.4%)	1 (2.8%)	9 (25.0%)	1 (2.8%)	36 (100%)
Lamas	2 (6.7%)	5 (16.7%)	22 (73.3%)	1 (3.3%)	30 (100%)
Ulcumayo	3 (10.7%)	9 (32.1%)	15 (53.6%)	1 (3.6%)	28 (100%)

Table 8. Language used by the father to address the child

Place of origin	Spanish	Quechua	Quechua and Spanish	Children without a father	Total
San Juan de Miraflores	26 (72.2%)	2 (5.6%)	7 (19.4%)	1 (2.8%)	36 (100%)
Lamas	3 (10%)	4 (13.3%)	23 (76.7%)	0 (0%)	30 (100%)
Ulcumayo	7 (25%)	5 (17.9%)	11 (39.3%)	5 (17.9%)	28 (100%)

With respect to the language used by the father to address the child, the perceptions of the three groups of children differed too. Table 8 reveals that in San Juan, 72.2% of the children reported that their fathers spoke to them in Spanish only, contrasting with 25% in Ulcumayo and a mere 10% in Lamas. Conversely, the percentages who reported that their fathers spoke to them only in Quechua were higher in Ulcumayo (17.9%) and Lamas (13.3%) than in San Juan (5.6%). The percentage of children who reported that their fathers spoke to them in both languages was highest in Lamas, 76.75%, 39.3% in Ulcumayo and lowest in San Juan, 19.4%.

In regard to the language used by siblings to address the children, the contrasts between the different geographical areas were even more marked. In San Juan, all of the children who had siblings claimed that their siblings spoke to them only in Spanish. This is indicative of the minimal exposure that these children have to Quechua and reveals the lack of prestige accorded to the language. The generational differences also reveal the fast pace of language shift in San Juan. In Lamas and in Ulcumayo, the majority of children (73.3% and 60.7% respectively) asserted that their siblings spoke to them in both languages. For both groups the second most frequent situation was to be spoken to only in Spanish (16.7% in Lamas and 28.6% in Ulcumayo).

Table 9. Language used by siblings to address the child

Place of origin	Spanish	Quechua	Quechua and Spanish	Children without siblings	Total
San Juan de Miraflores	31 (86.1%)	0 (0%)	0 (0%)	5 (13.9%)	36 (100%)
Lamas	5 (16.7%)	3 (10%)	22 (73.3%)	0 (0%)	30 (100%)
Ulcumayo	8 (28.6%)	2 (7.1%)	17 (60.7%)	1 (3.6%)	28 (100%)

Table 10. Language used by grandmother to address the child

Place of origin	Spanish	Quechua	Quechua and Spanish	Children without a grandmother	Total
San Juan de Miraflores	8 (22.2%)	4 (11.1%)	6 (16.7%)	18 (50.0%)	36 (100%)
Lamas	0 (0%)	10 (33.3%)	13 (43.3%)	7 (23.3%)	30 (100%)
Ulcumayo	2 (7.1%)	13 (46.4%)	9 (32.1%)	4 (14.3%)	28 (100%)

The information on language used by grandmothers also shows a pattern typical of language shift situations. In San Juan, up to 50% of the children do not have grandmothers or their grandmothers do not live with them, and 22% of those who have them reported that their grandmothers spoke to them only in Spanish, as shown in Table 10. In Lamas, no child reported that his or her grandmother spoke to her/him only in Spanish, and in Ulcumayo only 2 children (7.1%) claimed this situation. These data indicate that grandmothers are more frequently the source of Quechua for the children in the bilingual rural communities. In fact, a high percentage of the children reported that their grandmothers spoke to them only in Quechua or in both languages. More interestingly, in each case there is a decrease across generations of Quechua use. This decline is consistent across all three groups. The differences among the groups reveal that this generational progression is much more advanced in the San Juan group.

The picture that emerges from these data is one in which exposure to Quechua at home is more frequent for the children living in the bilingual rural communities than for the children living in the Spanish-dominant urban community of San Juan. Based on the information provided by the children I elaborated three tables that show the main patterns of language used by relatives to address the child in the household.

In San Juan, three groups emerged. The first one was constituted by 14 children who were addressed only in Spanish by their parents and siblings despite having at least one parent or caretaker who is bilingual in Quechua and Spanish. The second group was composed of 7 children. They were addressed in both languages by their mother or father. The third group had 15 children. These children were addressed in both languages by different relatives living in their households.

The patterns that emerged from Lamas and Ulcumayo reveal the extent of the bilingual input. In Lamas, two groups were distinguishable. The children in

Table 11. Patterns of linguistic input at home San Juan (Spanish-dominant community)

Groups	Mother	Father	Siblings	Grand-mother	Grand-father	Uncle	Aunt	Number of cases
I	S	S	S	X	X	X	X	8 (22.2%)
	S	S	S	S	X	X	X	3 (8.3%)
	S	S	S	S	S	X	X	2 (5.6%)
	S	S	S	S	X	S	X	1 (2.8%)
	Sub-total							14 (38.9%)
II	QS	QS	S	X	X	X	X	4 (11.1%)
	QS	QS	S	Q	X	X	X	1 (2.8%)
	QS	S	S	X	X	X	X	1 (2.8%)
	QS	S	S	X	X	S	X	1 (2.8%)
	Sub-total							7 (19.4%)
III	Other cases							15 (41.7%)
	Subtotal							15 (41.7%)
Total								36 (100%)

Group I were addressed by their bilingual relatives in the two languages and the children in Group II were addressed only in Spanish or only in Quechua by some of their relatives. Unlike in the case of San Juan, there is no core group of speakers who were addressed only in Spanish or Quechua.

In Ulcumayo, as in Lamas, two groups were distinguishable. The children in Group I were addressed by their bilingual relatives in the two languages and

Table 12. Patterns of linguistic input, Lamas (bilingual community)

Groups	Mother	Father	Sibling	Grand-mother	Grand-father	Uncle	Aunt	Number of cases
I	QS	QS	QS	QS	QS	QS	QS	8 (25.8%)
	QS	QS	QS	QS	QS	X	X	4 (12.9%)
	QS	QS	QS	QS	QS	QS	QS	1 (3.2%)
	Subtotal							13 (41.9%)
II	Other cases							18 (58.1%)
Total								31 (100%)

Table 13. Patterns of linguistic input at home, Ulcumayo (bilingual community)

Groups	Mother	Father	Siblings	Grand-mother	Grand-father	Uncle	Aunt	Number of cases
I	QS	QS	QS	QS	QS	QS	QS	8 (28.6%)
	QS	S	QS	QS	QS	QS	QS	1 (3.6%)
	QS	QS	QS	Q	QS	QS	QS	1 (3.6%)
	QS	QS	QS	QS	X	QS	QS	1 (3.6%)
	QS	QS	S	QS	QS	QS	QS	1 (3.6%)
	Sub-total							12 (42.9%)
II	Other cases							16 (57.1%)
Total								28 (100%)

the children in Group II were addressed only in Spanish or only in Quechua by some of their relatives. Again, there was no core group of speakers who were addressed only in Spanish.

3.4 Patterns of linguistic input at school

In terms of the patterns of linguistic input at school, I asked the children about the language they used to speak to their peers and to the teacher in the classroom. A clear difference emerged between San Juan de Miraflores on the one hand and Lamas and Ulcumayo on the other. The data summarized in Table 14 show that none of the children in the Spanish-dominant community of San Juan reported using Quechua in the classroom. In Lamas, where the children are part of a bilingual education program, 46.67% of the children reported speaking only in Spanish, while 23.33% claimed to speak only in Quechua and 30% in the two languages. Circumstances favored Spanish in Ulcumayo where no bilingual education program is in place. There, 75% of the children reported speaking only in Spanish, while 14.29% claimed to speak only in Quechua, and 10.71% in both languages.

No child in San Juan reported that their teachers spoke in Quechua to them. In Ulcumayo, where no bilingual program is in place, 89.29% of the children reported that their teachers addressed them only in Spanish (compare with their 75% usage). In Lamas, the children's responses reflected their perception that the teacher often uses the native language in the classroom. The

Table 14. Language used in the classroom

Place of origin	Spanish	Quechua	Quechua and Spanish	Total
San Juan de Miraflores	36 (100%)	0 (0%)	0 (0%)	36 (100%)
Lamas	14 (46.67%)	7 (23.33%)	9 (30%)	30 (100%)
Ulcumayo	21 (75%)	4 (14.29%)	3 (10.71%)	28 (100%)

Lamas, Ulcumayo chi-square test $p<0.0760$

more frequent use of Quechua by both students and teachers reveals the relative esteem enjoyed by the language in this community. In Lamas there are noticeably more efforts to incorporate the language into the classroom.

Table 15. Language used in classroom by the teacher

Place of origin	Spanish	Quechua	Quechua and Spanish	Total
San Juan de Miraflores	36 (100%)	0 (0%)	0 (0%)	36 (0%)
Lamas	10 (33.33%)	8 (26.67%)	12 (40%)	30 (100%)
Ulcumayo	25 (89.29)	1 (3.57%)	2 (7.14%)	28 (100%)

Chi-square test $p<0.0001$

These data clearly indicate that the children in the San Juan group receive considerably less Quechua input overall, and those in the Ulcumayo group receives less Quechua input at school than the Lamas group.

To summarize, I have presented the three groups of children that participated in this study. The group in San Juan belongs to an urban community where Spanish is the dominant language, and where the use of Quechua is restricted to domestic environments. Their exposure to input in Quechua is reduced at home and virtually non-existent at school.

The group from Lamas belongs to a rural community. Although the community is experiencing language shift from Quechua to Spanish, it has the highest ratio of Quechua speakers to Spanish speakers of the three groups. Additionally, local representatives are struggling to maintain the native language, perhaps as a result of their unique status as speakers of an Andean language in an Amazonian region. These community leaders also possess a strong sense of pride in their cultural identity. The children that participated in this study receive input in Quechua and Spanish at home and also at school, and many of them have grandparents who are Quechua-Spanish bilinguals.

The group from Ulcumayo belongs to a rural community, but, unlike their Lamas counterpart, this community is not an isolated Quechua-speaking population, since it is situated in a geographical continuum in the Central Andes where Spanish is replacing Quechua. It has a higher ratio of Quechua speakers to Spanish speakers than the San Juan community but a lower ratio than Lamas. The children who participated in this study receive input in the two languages at home, and are exposed to much less input in Quechua at school than the Lamas group. Many of them have grandparents who are Quechua-Spanish bilinguals, a situation that mirrors that of the children from Lamas. This situation of multiple generations of bilinguals is crucial to my research question, as it allows for the observation of the long-term effects of language contact on the grammar of Quechua and Spanish with respect to the direct object system and it addresses the issue of a community of speakers in which constant activation of the two languages takes place.

3.5 Measuring linguistic knowledge of bilinguals in a language shift situation

Given the complexity of the language contact situation just described, several techniques were tried to elicit comparable data from the children.[6] A pilot study was conducted in San Juan and Lamas to explore the most appropriate techniques for data elicitation. The results of that pilot are reported in Sanchez (2002). The techniques that proved more successful in the first approximation to the children were a picture-based story telling task and a picture–sentence matching task.[7] These two techniques, in particular, the first one, worked well because although the participants were literate, they were not familiar with testing situations or with experimental testing. This was particularly true of our two bilingual rural groups. Additionally, written grammaticality judgment tasks were not used because of the difficulty of their use among populations with low levels of literacy.

---

6. A general questionnaire preceded the application of the data collection tools. The questionnaire included questions on the children's general data (age, grade, sex) their age of exposure to the two languages, and their language preferences at home and in school as well as those of their relatives and teachers.

7. A pre-test using elicited imitation was conducted among the three groups but its results were random and could not be used for any purposes.

Data for this study were elicited using two tasks: a picture-based story telling task that provides information on discourse antecedents for the clitic structures involved and a picture–sentence matching task that allows for control of the topic antecedents of the structures analyzed. Oral bilingual Quechua data were elicited using the picture-based story-telling task.[8] However, the picture–sentence matching task was not used for Quechua due to the low levels of Quechua literacy among the children.

3.5.1 Picture-based story-telling task

For the picture-based story-telling task, the participants observed a series of 18 pictures (see examples in Appendix I) in which a story based on Mayer and Mayer's (1992) frog story is depicted.[9] The sequence presents a child who is surrounded by his three pet animals: a turtle, a frog and a dog. He receives a package and opens it and inside there is a little frog. The story evolves as the big frog experiences jealousy and the child and animals are involved in various adventures in the countryside leading to the little frog's disappearance and subsequent re-encounter with all the characters.

This task was selected because it was culturally appropriate for the populations studied, as they were all familiar with the types of animals depicted, the environment and the relationships between children and animals. The limited number of actions depicted that required the use of transitive verbs made control over the number of verbs manageable. A fixed number of characters in the story made control of overt DPs, pronouns, clitic constructions and their antecedents also manageable.

3.5.2 Picture-sentence matching task

The picture–sentence matching task consisted of a series of 11 pictures, followed by a question related to the story and pictures, then two possible answers

---

8. The data for the pilot study were collected in San Martin in 1998 and the data for the study reported in this book were collected in 1999.
9. The pictures were based on Mayer's (1969) story, however, the images and the story lines were significantly changed to be culturally appropriate for the populations that participated in this study. For example, Figure 10 in Appendix I includes high mountains as an adaptation to the geography of Junin and a wooden raft of the type most likely to be recognized by the children Lamas instead of a boat.

to the question (see examples in Appendix II).[10] The interviewers read the question and the answers out loud and the children were allowed to read them. Then the interviewers asked the children to select the answer that they thought was more appropriate. The answers did not differ with respect to their semantic content, but rather with respect to the grammatical structures used. The questions and answers in this task are discussed in Chapter 5.

This task was selected in order to probe into the grammatical knowledge of children outside of discourse conditions. It was intended to check the children's grammatical preferences when the topic/focus structure of the answer was predicted by the question.

3.5.3 Conditions for data elicitation

The data were elicited in the children's schools by a group of research assistants. In the area of Ulcumayo we (a total of three research assistants and I) interviewed the children individually. The interviews in Ulcumayo proper took place in the school principal's office or in a classroom and took approximately five days to be completed. In Apán, a *caserío* near Ulcumayo, interviews also took place in the principal's office and in an empty classroom, and were conducted in one day.

In Lamas, we (a total of five research assistants and I) interviewed the children. Most interviews took place in the principal's office and some took place in the school's library and in empty classrooms. They took approximately three days.

In Ulcumayo and San Juan, the research assistants were not members of the community. They had some knowledge of Quechua as a second language and one was a native speaker of the language.

In San Juan de Miraflores, we (four research assistants and I) conducted the interviews over a period of three days. Interviews took place in the vice-principal's office and in some cases in the halls outside the classrooms, as the library was not available and there were no empty classrooms.

For the picture-based story telling task, the children were asked in Spanish to look at the pictures first and afterwards they were asked to narrate the story first in the language that they considered their native language and immediately after that they were asked to narrate the story in the other language.[11]

---

10. There was another question that had no picture associated to it. This question is not included in this report as it was not understood by many of the participants.
11. Most of them were bilingual from birth but still chose one of the two languages.

After narrating the story the children were shown the pictures associated to the picture-sentence matching task and provided their answers. The entire session was audio recorded and the interviewers wrote the responses the to the matching task on an answer sheet.[12] Interviews lasted between 30 and 45 minutes.

Finally, the data was transcribed[13] and coded by two research assistants in the case of Quechua and by 5 research assistants in the case of Spanish, under my supervision in both cases. For each language, a different a set of guidelines were used. Additionally, for Quechua a list of suffixes (see Appendix III), a coding sheet and a list of code numbers were distributed among codifiers. For Spanish, a coding sheet and a list of code numbers were used.

To summarize, in this chapter I have presented the main sociolinguistic characteristics of the children interviewed for this study as well as of the communities where they live in order to make explicit the type of language contact and language shift situations in which they live. The bilinguals who participated in this study have had access to both languages at home and at school as well as in the community. They activate both languages frequently. Language contact in their communities is also characterized by language shift to the prestigious language, Spanish. This background is needed to understand that some of the evidence in favor of the Functional Interference Hypothesis and the Functional Convergence Hypothesis that will be discussed later, for instance evidence of convergence towards some uses of Quechua null direct object pronouns, cannot be attributed to a social preference for Quechua over Spanish in their communities. At the same time, evidence of the convergence towards some specific Spanish functional features and not towards others will be analyzed in light of their activation in discourse and not necessarily in terms of a general prestige associated to Spanish.

I have also presented the data collection and coding techniques that were used in the study. These were tested prior to the study for their adequacy to the levels of literacy of the populations studied as well as for their cultural relevance to the participants.

---

12. Electronic versions of the recordings in MP3 files are available from the author and are linked to www.rci.rutgers.edu/~lsanchez. WAV files are also available from the author upon request.

13. Electronic files with the transcriptions are also available from the author and will be linked to www.rci.rutgers.edu/~lsanchez

CHAPTER 4

A turtle is looking at *a* toad
Functional interference and convergence in bilingual Quechua

4.1 Story-telling task results in bilingual Quechua

As presented in Chapter 1, the Functional Interference Hypothesis predicts that, in the minds of bilinguals who activate both languages constantly, interference in functional features results in syntactic changes in the bilingual grammar. On the other hand, the Functional Convergence Hypothesis predicts that such constant activation may result in a common specification for equivalent functional categories in the two languages.

In this chapter, I will present evidence from the story-telling task in Quechua that supports the Functional Interference and the Functional Convergence hypotheses. Only the bilingual participants performed this task in Quechua. The participants in San Juan did not perform this part of the story-telling task because of their very limited knowledge of Quechua. The task had as its main goal the elicitation of sentences containing transitive verbs and direct object complements, such as full DPs, direct object null pronouns and strong or demonstrative pronouns as well as the elicitation of sentences with various word orders. In order to test the Functional Interference Hypothesis and the Functional Convergence Hypothesis, an analysis of transitive verbs and their complements was conducted. I expected to find evidence of interference and convergence in the functional features under D and Cl. Indeed, this was clearly the case for D features in one of the two bilingual groups. General tendencies towards convergence in the functional features of Cl were found in the two groups, evidenced by a high frequency in SVO word orders. There was also dropping of the accusative marker *-ta* which I will propose is related to changes in the D feature system.

In the Quechua narratives, some instances of Spanish lexical borrowings for verbs and nouns were found. These indicate some interference with respect to lexical entries. However, their low percentage does not compete with the higher frequency of phenomena that are evidence in favor of syntactic changes due to interference in the specification of functional features and that confirm the Functional Interference Hypothesis.

There were also instances of code-switching into Spanish at different constituent levels such as VPs and IPs. These were cases in which Spanish clitics appeared inside Spanish IP islands. A detailed analysis of switches inside IP will be presented in this chapter to demonstrate that these may also be indicative of constant activation leading to interference and convergence in functional categories.

This chapter is organized as follows. First, the distribution of the verbal lexical items in the Quechua narratives is presented to show a similarity in the type of data collected for the two groups and to attest to the level of lexical interference between the two languages. Second, the distribution of direct objects is presented to establish the frequency with which overt DPs and other pronominal forms (overt or null) were used in this oral task in Quechua. These data will be compared to the results of the same task in Spanish in Chapter 5 in order to find evidence in favor of interference and convergence in the functional features associated to D. Third, evidence for functional convergence in D and Cl from accusative case dropping, SVO word order and the emergence of an indefinite determiner in the Quechua narratives will be presented and discussed. Finally, data on the topic relations of direct object pronominal forms with their antecedents in discourse will be discussed to further investigate their role in acting as clues guiding interference and convergence in functional features in D and Cl.

4.1.1 Consistency in the type of verbs used in the narratives

All transitive verbs were coded. The bilingual group in Ulcumayo produced a higher number of verbs, as shown in Table 1. Variation among speakers was also greater in Ulcumayo than in Lamas, as evidenced by the standard deviation.

In analyzing verb production, a distinction was made between verb tokens and verb types. Every instance of production of a verb was counted as a verb token. A lexical item was counted as a verb type. Thus, 10 occurrences of the same lexical item were counted as 10 tokens and 1 type. The bilingual children in Ulcumayo produced more verb types and tokens than the bilingual children in Lamas, despite the additional exposure of the latter group to Quechua in school. Comparing the results of this task in Spanish, the bilingual children in Lamas produced fewer verb tokens and verb types in Quechua than in Spanish,

Table 1. Number of verbs in Quechua narratives

	Ulcumayo	Lamas
Average	25.5	17.7
Standard deviation	16.5	9.9
Max	67.0	45
Min	1.0	1
Total	714	512

Table 2. Distribution of tokens and types of Quechua verbs

	Lamas	Ulcumayo
Token	512	714
Type	63	100
Variability	0.123	0.140

while the group in Ulcumayo produced more verb tokens and types in Quechua than in Spanish (see Chapter 5). The distribution of the actual lexical items in the Quechua narratives of Lamas and Ulcumayo can be found in Appendix IV.

There was a high number of verb types used only once in the narratives. At the same time, the number of verb types lowered when the number of tokens increased. The most common verb type for Lamas was the verb *qaway* 'to look.' Its Spanish-rooted counterpart *mirar* 'to look' was also very frequent and the verb *apiy* 'to bring/carry' was also very frequent. Among the most frequent verb types were *markay* 'to cradle' and the Spanish-rooted *apuntay* 'to point'. A similar pattern of verb token/type ratio was found in the Ulcumayo data. As in the case of the narratives from Lamas, the verbs *rirgay* 'mirar' and its Spanish-rooted counterpart *miray* 'mirar' were among the most frequent. The same was true of the forms *chariy* 'to catch' and their Spanish-rooted counterpart *agarrar* 'to grab.' Thus, despite some differences in the range of verb types used by the children in both groups, the most common types fell under the same lexical areas.

Another important aspect of the distribution of verbs in the Quechua narratives of the two groups was the percentage of Spanish roots. An example of cases in which a Spanish root was part of a Quechua verb is given in (1):[1]

---

1. I did not include in the analysis auxiliary verbs that may have been expressed in Spanish, in order to avoid the complication of counting them as transitive verbs.

Ulcumayo (Participant U4)
(1) **Alsa**-ru-n.
 raise-PAST-3SG
 'S/he raises'

For both groups the percentage of Spanish roots was similar. Similar frequencies of verbal borrowings from Spanish (23% for Ulcumayo and 24.7% for Lamas) were found. I take this low frequency to indicate that despite language shift and language contact, this area of the lexicon has not been severely affected by interference.

Table 3. Quechua and Spanish verbal roots in Quechua narratives

Verbal roots	Ulcumayo		Lamas	
Quechua	550	(77.0%)	388	(75.8%)
Spanish	164	(23.0%)	124	(24.2%)
Total	714	(100.0%)	512	(100.0%)

Chi-square test $p < 0.611$

I found a high frequency of Quechua roots with Quechua inflections (person, gerund or infinitival morphemes) for both groups as shown on Table 4. The following examples illustrate the case of Quechua verbs inflected with Quechua suffixes:

Lamas (Participant L4)
(2) Chay motelo qawa-n chay sapu-ta.
 that turtle see-3SG that toad-ACC
 'That turtle sees that toad'

Ulcumayo (Participant U13)
(3) Saputa[2] rirga-ya-n wambracha-ta.
 toad see-DUR-3SG boy-ACC
 'The toad sees the turtle'

---

2. In the speech of several children in Ulcumayo and Lamas, there were subjects followed by a *-ta* suffix. The context provided by the images confirmed them as subjects. They had a definite antecedent. It would appear as though this *-ta* is some form of a post-nominal determiner. I did not find a reference to a *-ta* suffix for subjects in the Quechua grammars consulted.

This shows that person and durative suffixes have not been affected greatly by contact.

There were, however, some instances of Quechua roots with Spanish inflection or without inflection. Their frequency was low in general and they were more frequent in Ulcumayo than in Lamas. Example (4) illustrates a case of Spanish inflection in a gerund form and example (5) illustrates the case of a null person inflection:

Ulcumayo (Participant U5)
(4) *Sapu*-qa taraya-n rirga-r-ando
toad-TOP sit-3s look-INF-GERUND
'The toad is sitting looking'

Ulcumayo (Participant U17)
(5) Tortuga rachakta rirga-ya-Ø.
turtle toad-ACC see-DUR-Ø
'The turtle sees the toad'

Out of the 20 cases of anomalous morphology reported in Ulcumayo, 19 correspond to cases of null person inflection. These can be interpreted as instances of morphological simplification on the Quechua verbal inflection. However, their low frequency does not allow for an analysis that favors a simplification in the inflectional morphology of the two varieties of Quechua in the contact situation.

Table 4. Verbal inflection of Quechua roots

Verbal inflection	Ulcumayo		Lamas	
Quechua	530	(96.4%)	383	(98.7%)
Ø, Spanish	20	(3.6%)	5	(1.3%)
Total	550	(100.0%)	388	(100.0%)

Chi-square test $p<0.028$

There is a higher frequency of Spanish roots with Quechua inflection than with Spanish inflection for both groups. This shows that there were more cases of Spanish borrowing at the noun level than cases of code-switching or constituent insertion at the VP-level.

Table 5 presents the number and percentage of Spanish roots with Quechua or Spanish inflection. None showed the omission of morphology. Example 6 illustrates the case of a Spanish root with Quechua inflection:

Lamas (Participant L1)
(6) Chay perro *mira*-ku-n.³
 that perro see-REFLEX-3SG
 'That dog sees'

Table 5. Verbal inflection of Spanish roots

Verbal inflection	Ulcumayo		Lamas	
Quechua	101	(61.6%)	98	(79.0%)
Spanish	63	(38.4%)	26	(21.0%)
Total	164	(100.0%)	124	(100.0%)

Chi-square test $p<0.0015$

The table shows that the percentage of Spanish roots with Spanish inflection is lower in Lamas than in Ulcumayo. They tend to occur in sentences in which some form of intra-sentential code-switching has occurred. The following example shows such a case taken from the frog stories, where the material in italics is in Spanish:

Lamas (Participant L1)
(7) Chay saputa *le bot-ó   a ese sapo*.
 that toad Cl throw-PAST-3SG to that toad
 'That toad pushed that toad'

In this example, the subject NP is in Quechua whereas the rest of the tensed clause is in Spanish.

Another indicator of a pattern of verb use similar among the groups was the frequency of discourse particles on the verbs. Table 6 shows that, in both bilingual samples, most of the verbs were not inflected with discourse particles. The narratives did not show examples of all the possible discourse particles that are listed in the descriptive grammars of both varieties (Parker 1976, Black, Bolli and Ticsi 1990, Coombs, Coombs and Weber 1976) as anticipated in Chapter 2. Dubitative particles such as *-cha* for Lamista Quechua, and *-tri* for

---

3. The suffix *-ku* is referred to in the grammars as the reflexive or middle passive suffix (Parker 1976), however, it may have other uses such as to indicate a special interest on the part of the agent (Black, Bolli and Ticsi Zarate 1990). In the context provided by the illustrations it does not have a reflexive meaning.

Table 6. Discourse affixes on verbs

Discourse affixes	Ulcumayo		Lamas	
No affix	689	(96.5%)	495	(96.7%)
With affix (evidential/focus/topic/other)*	25	(3.5%)	17	(3.3%)
Total	714	(100.0%)	512	(100.0%)

Chi-square test $p < 0.864$
* -mi/-m/-n, -ka/-qa/, -si/-s, -ta, -ya/-lla/-yu

Ulcumayo Quechua were not found. These frequencies indicate that, in the type of discourse analyzed, verbs tend to not be focalized, and that most of the topic/focus contrasts fell on nominal arguments. Probably, the sequence of pictures used to elicit the data forced a fixed number of referents that were introduced and re-introduced as discourse topics. These were expressed as nominal elements (DPs, overt and null pronouns) and they carried most of the topic/focus markers.

To summarize, in this section, I have shown that the narratives from the two groups had similar frequencies in the distribution of Quechua and Spanish verbal roots as well as in the distribution of inflection morphemes and discourse markers. I have also shown that convergence at the lexical level involving verb roots and person morphemes is not statistically high. In Subsection 4.1.3, evidence of changes in other areas of the morphology that show variability in functional features will be shown, which provide support to the Functional Interference Hypothesis.

4.1.2 Distribution of direct objects in bilingual Quechua

In order to investigate the differences or similarities in the feature specification of D in the bilingual narratives an analysis of the frequencies of direct object complements was performed. It shows a higher frequency of DPs than any other direct object complement. The following examples illustrate a case of a full DP in direct object position:

Ulcumayo (Participant U 22)
(8) Huk wambra # racha-kta chari-ya-n.
     a   boy   toad-ACC grab-DUR-3SG
     'A boy is holding a toad'

Table 7 shows the results of the frequency analysis.[4] DPs with Quechua or Spanish noun roots are the most frequent type of complement in the Quechua narratives of both bilingual groups (55.9% in Ulcumayo, 60.6% in Lamas). The high frequency of DPs may indicate that this particular task elicited DPs as the first reference to the direct objects in the story. Notice also that, as in the case of verbal roots, the frequency of Spanish noun roots was not high either, indicating again that convergence is not taking place in that area of the lexicon in a statistically significant pattern.

The second most frequent type of direct object complement is represented by null pronouns in the narratives of both groups. The following example illustrates a null pronoun complement:

Lamas (Participant L14)
(9) Chay niñito apunta-yka-n   chay sapito$_i$.
     that boy   point-DUR-3SG that toad$_i$
     'That boy points at that toad'

(10) Chay tortuga pro$_i$ kawa-rka-n   piñaku-shka-na
     that turtle pro$_i$ look-PAST-3SG upset-DUR-NOM
     'That turtle looked (at him) upset'

In sentence (10) there is a null direct object complement that refers to the toad that the boy is pointing at according to sentence (9) (see Figure 6). This is a clear example of a null pronoun that refers to a previously mentioned DP that is definite and specific.

The narratives of the two groups show very low frequencies of demonstrative or strong pronouns and direct object complement CPs. The following examples illustrate the three types of direct object complements:

Strong Pronoun. Ulcumayo (Participant U7)
(11) Kaychun chari-ya-n   hukta.
     here   grab-DUR-3SG other
     'Here (he) is grabbing the other one'

---

4. This table does not include the cases in which the direct object complement involved a Spanish clitic. There were very few instances of clitics (9 in the Ulcumayo narratives and 5 in the Lamas narratives). Each instance will be discussed individually later in this section.

Demonstrative Pronoun. Ulcumayo (Participant U13)
(12) Kayta rirga-ya-n.
 this one see-DUR-3SG
 '(He) is looking at this one'

CP. Ulcumayo (Participant U24)
(13) Chari-y-ta muna-ya-n.
 grab-INF-ACC want-DUR-3SG
 '(He) wants to grab'

The lack of strong pronouns and demonstrative pronouns is consistent with the fact that most of the direct object complements were topics and overt strong pronouns and demonstratives tend to be focused elements in Quechua. As mentioned in Chapter 2, given the sharp differences between CP complements in Quechua and Spanish, their extremely low frequency was also expected. Overall, the frequencies of direct object complements for both groups were higher for DPs followed by null objects with definite and/or specific antecedents and there was a very low frequency of strong pronouns or demonstratives.[5]

Table 7. Direct object complements

Direct object complements in Quechua narratives	Ulcumayo		Lamas	
Quechua DP	330	(46.8%)	287	(56.6%)
Spanish DP	64	(9.1%)	18	(3.6%)
Complex DP	20	(2.8%)	25	(4.9%)
Null	273	(38.7%)	173	(34.1%)
Quechua Strong Pronoun	3	(0.4%)	0	(0.0%)
Demonstrative Pronoun (Quechua or Spanish)	13	(1.8%)	1	(0.2%)
CP (Quechua or Spanish)	2	(0.3%)	3	(0.6%)
Total	705	(100.0%)	507	(100.0%)

Chi-square test, $p < 0.000$

Some instances of Spanish clitics attached to Quechua verbal forms were found in the narratives in Quechua. In the Ulcumayo narratives, a total of nine sentences with clitics were found, and in Lamas there were only five. Although very low in frequency, their presence may be indicative of activation of the two languages in the same sentential structure. Another possibility is to analyze

---

5. Notice also that there is a slightly higher frequency of null objects in Ulcumayo than in Lamas, as seen in Table 7.

them as frozen forms that are treated by the bilingual speakers as unanalyzed units. This latter possibility seems to be ruled out by the fact that they occur with different verbs and verbal tenses. In most cases, they appeared in contexts in which a switch to Spanish had taken place, and they seem to have been favored by participants with a tendency to switch to Spanish. The cases from Ulcumayo involved six participants. The Spanish forms are in italics:

Ulcumayo (Participant U7)
(14) *La* char*ido*.
 Cl held
 '(S/he) held it'

Ulcumayo (Participant U17)
(15) Rachakta *miro-le al*   # wambra # *la*   *tortuga tam(b)ién*.
 toad-ACC see-Cl to-the boy   the turtle too
 'The toad looked at the boy, the turtle did too'

Ulcumayo (Participant U20)
(16) *La pegadu*ta chiksanayla *sapu*-ta.
 Cl hit   small little toad-ACC
 '(S/he, it) has beaten the little toad'

(17) *Al* *niñu*-ta *la botó*   *al* chiksanayla *sapu*-laq.
 to the boy-ACC Cl knocked over to-the little   toad-RESTRICTIVE
 'The little boy knocked over the little toad'

(18) Chiksanayla *sapu*-la   *le ha pegado*.
 little   toad-RESTRICTIVE Cl has beaten
 '(S/he, it) has beaten the little toad'

(19) *Sapu*ta *la botó*   *al* chiksanayla *sapo*.
 toad Cl knocked over to-the little   toad
 'The toad knocked over the little toad'

Ulcumayo (Participant U18)
(20) *El* algo *le mira*.
 the dog Cl sees
 'The dog sees him/it'

Ulcumayo (Participant U16)
(21) ⟨kay⟩ [/] kay wambra *la &*aga *la agarró al*   *sapo*.
      that boy Cl &ca... Cl catched to-the toad
 'That boy catched the toad'

Ulcumayo (Participant U21)
(22) ⟨*ranas*⟩ [/] *ranas le botó   este.*
     frogs   frogs Cl knocked over this
     'This one knocked over the frog'

The form *la* 'feminine clitic' appears five times in Ulcumayo although in cases such as (14) it can be interpreted as a contraction of a clitic initial consonant *l-* from either *le* 'dative clitic' or *lo* 'masculine accusative clitic' and the auxiliary verb *ha* 'has' in a Spanish present perfect verb form. The sequence *la charido* can be interpreted as *le/lo/la ha charido* 'has held it' (dative/accusative masculine/accusative feminine). In Ulcumayo, clitics appeared more frequently in clitic doubling constructions as in sentences (15), (17) and (19) with Spanish inflected verbs. It is clear that in these cases, the verb and the clitic form a Spanish constituent. Additionally, the direct object is preceded by the Spanish preposition *a* indicating a Spanish functional head. Most of the clitic sentences have null subjects or Spanish DPs in subject position except for (15) in which the subject is clearly a Quechua DP.

In Lamas, clitic constructions were found in the narratives of three participants. One of them had a clitic doubling construction. As in the case of Ulcumayo, three cases appeared in the narrative of a participant that tended to switch to Spanish (see participant L1 below). The three cases were sentences in which VP-internal material appeared also in Spanish indicating VP-insertion. The form *la* was absent in the Quechua narratives from Lamas and only the form *le* was found.

Lamas (Participant L1)
(23) Chay *sapo le pateó # abajo.*
     that toad Cl kicked down
     'That toad kicked it down'

(24) Chay ⟨*niñu*ta⟩ [/] *niñu*ta # ne # ne # *le (es)tá queriendo matar.*
     that ⟨boy⟩   boy   eh   eh   Cl is wanting to kill
     'That boy wants to kill him'

(25) # Chay *sapu*ta # *le botó   a ese sapo.*
          that toad   Cl knocked over to that toad
     'That toad knocked over that toad'

Lamas (Participant L7)
(26) Suk *perro # ta # cariñándo-le a su niñito.*
     a   dog   is   caressing-Cl to his boy
     'A dog is caressing his boy'

Lamas (Participant L20)
(27) Chay motelo chayrayku *le hace caminar*.
that turtle therefore Cl makes walk
'Therefore that turtle makes him walk'

All of these can be analyzed as cases of VP-insertion in code-mixing of the type described by Muysken (2000). All of the clitics are associated with Spanish verbs or Spanish verb inflection in the nine cases in Ulcumayo and in the five cases in Lamas.

In general, the distribution of direct objects in the Quechua narratives from the two groups shows a higher frequency of overt DPs followed by null pronouns and a very low frequency of overt demonstrative or strong pronouns and CP complements. Additionally, some evidence of activation of two languages in the same sentence was found in six participants in Lamas and three in Ulcumayo. These data will be compared to the results obtained for the same task in Spanish in Chapter 5.

4.1.3 Evidence for functional convergence: The dropping of accusative marking, the emergence of overt D, and SVO word order

Looking more specifically at the frequencies of DPs in direct object positions in the Quechua narratives, I analyzed the morphological markings for case. In Chapter 2, data from Ulcumayo Quechua and Lamas Quechua grammars were presented that show that the two varieties mark direct object DPs for case with the accusative marker *-ta*. This affix marker was found in the narratives (see examples (2) and (3)) but there were also cases of the dropped accusative marker *-ta*, particularly in the narratives from Lamas (see example (9)). Table 8 shows the results for morphological markings on DP direct object complements.[6]

The table shows a strong difference between Lamas and Ulcumayo in the percentage of direct object DPs with a Quechua root that are morphologically unmarked for accusative case. The narratives from Lamas had 55.4% of Quechua DPs unmarked for case whereas the narratives from Ulcumayo had only 10.9%. I take this to indicate that the Lamas Quechua morphological case system is evolving towards a system in which the accusative marker *-ta* is being dropped. Accusative dropping is a marked phenomenon in other varieties of

---

6. The data in this table does not include DP direct object complements that were preceded by the Spanish preposition *a* that marks animate/specific direct objects.

Table 8. Accusative markers on DPs

Direct object	Accusative marker	Lamas		Ulcumayo	
DP (Q)	Ø	173	(55.4%)	44	(10.9%)
	-ta	109	(34.9%)	283	(70.2%)
DP (S)	Ø	5	(1.6%)	37	(9.2%)
	-ta	1	(0.3%)	19	(4.7%)
Complex DP(Q)	Ø	10	(3.2%)	5	(1.2%)
	-ta	14	(4.5%)	15	(3.7%)
Total		312	(100.0%)	403	(100.0%)

Chi-square test $p<0.000$

Quechua, particularly since the L1 acquisition data analyzed by Courtney (1998) and presented in Chapter 2 show evidence of early accusative marking. It is also marked given the fact that -*ta* is used not only as an accusative marker but also as an objective marker, that is, a marker for other NPs inside VP, as discussed in Chapter 2. Notice also that, although there were fewer Spanish DPs in Lamas than in Ulcumayo, these were mostly unmarked for accusative case. This situation is similar to the few cases of accusative marker dropping found by Courtney (1998), in which accusative case-markers were dropped for Spanish loan words.

In Ulcumayo, almost a third of the Spanish DPs were marked for accusative case, indicating that lexical borrowings are subject to the requirements of a still robust morphological case system.

The difference between the frequencies of accusative marking on the DPs cannot be attributed to differences in the frequencies of complex DPs[7] as Table 9 shows.

---

7. These are DPs involving some form of coordination.

Table 9. Accusative marking on complex DPs[8]

Direct object	Accusative marker	Lamas		Ulcumayo	
Complex DP(Q)	∅	10	(41.7%)	5	(25.0%)
	-ta	14	(58.3%)	15	(75.0%)
Total		24	(100.0%)	20	(100.0%)

Chi-square test $p<0.245$

I also looked at the morphological markings on null and strong pronouns and on CP complements. The Ulcumayo data show three strong pronouns and one demonstrative pronoun marked for accusative case. No cases of either strong or demonstrative pronouns were found in Lamas. There was only one Spanish and one Quechua CP and the latter was marked for accusative in the Ulcumayo data (see example 13).

One possible explanation for the lack of overt accusative marking in the Lamas narratives is that the Spanish preposition *a* that marks animacy and specificity in direct objects in Spanish (Jaeggli 1986) has become part of the Lamas bilingual grammatical system and is used to mark accusative case. As mentioned in Chapter 2, this preposition appears at the early stages of L1 Spanish acquisition and could be interpreted and used as a case marker by the bilingual children. This is not a plausible account for two reasons. First, the preposition *a* may coexist with the accusative marker in the speech of some children as shown in:

    Lamas (Participant L7)
(28) Suk motelo kawa-yka-n   a ese niñitu-ta.
      a   turtle look-DUR-3SG to that boy-ACC
      'A turtle is looking at that little boy'

Second, the frequency of *a* is low in the narratives of both groups; there are no significant differences between them, as shown in Table 10.

Thus, the high frequency of dropping of the accusative marker *-ta* in Lamas cannot be correlated to the presence of the Spanish preposition *a*. As we will see in the next subsection, accusative dropping in Lamas Quechua co-occurs with the emergence of an indefinite determiner and appears to be closely related to change in the feature specification of D.

---

8. This table also excludes direct object complements that were preceded by the Spanish preposition *a*.

Table 10. Direct object marking with Spanish preposition *a*

Preposition *a*	Ulcumayo		Lamas	
Lacking preposition *a*	698	(97.8%)	503	(98.2%)
Preceded by preposition *a*	16	(2.2%)	9	(1.8%)
Total	714	(100.0%)	518	(100.0%)

Chi-square test $p<0.555$

4.1.3.1 Emergence of an indefinite determiner

As mentioned in Chapter 2, most varieties of Quechua, including Lamas and Ulcumayo lack overt pre-nominal determiners.[9] However, definiteness and indefiniteness are occasionally expressed through pre-nominal demonstrative adjectives such as *kay* 'this' and the numeral *huk/suk* 'one', respectively. In analyzing the data from the narratives, three possibilities for the coding of definiteness were considered: absence of a pre-nominal determiner, presence of a pre-nominal demonstrative adjective with a definite interpretation, and presence of the numeral *huk* 'one' in Ulcumayo or *suk* 'one' in Lamas with an indefinite interpretation.[10] The following examples illustrate those cases:

Lack of Determiner. Ulcumayo (Participant U26)
(29) Chari-ya-n   agash-ta.
      grab-DUR-3SG toad-ACC
      '(He) grabs the toad'

Definite Demonstrative. Lamas (Participant L13)
(30) Chaymanta **chay** wambriyo # *mira*-rka-n   ⟨chay sapu⟩ [//] **chay**
      then   that   boy   # look-PAST-3SG ⟨that   toad⟩ [//] that
      sapu-ta.
      toad-ACC
      'Then, that boy looked at that toad'

---

9. I refer to determiners that are not of a suffix nature. It has been argued that some Central varieties of Quechua exhibit a post-nominal suffix that can be interpreted as a determiner (Cerron-Palomino 1987) and below I will refer to some proposals according to which the accusative suffix *-ta* has some definiteness features associated to it.

10. In some cases of complex DPs such as coordinates, it was difficult to determine the definiteness of the whole DP. If at least an overt definite DP was involved it was coded as definite. However in Ulcumayo some cases remained obscure and they were coded as difficult to determine.

Indefinite numeral. Lamas (Participant L7)
(31) **Suk** motelo mira-yka-n   ⟨suk sapitu-ta⟩ [/] **suk** &sa # sapitu-ta.
       a   turtle look-DUR-3SG ⟨a   toad-ACC⟩ [/] a   &to # toad-ACC
       'A turtle is looking at a toad'

The Lamas narratives showed a low frequency of bare NPs in object position compared to the frequency of DPs with demonstratives and the indefinite numeral indicating a pattern of convergence with the DP grammar of Spanish that requires an overt D with definite and indefinite noun phrases in object position provided that they are not generic.[11] The Ulcumayo narratives had a higher percentage of bare nouns than the Lamas data; the sharpest contrast between the narratives from Lamas and Ulcumayo was found in the use of overt indefinite determiners. These were significantly more frequent in Lamas than in Ulcumayo.

Table 11. Definite and indefinite determiners on DPs (Q and S)

DPs	Ulcumayo	Lamas
Bare NP	244 (58.9%)	76 (23.0%)
Demonstrative (definite)	150 (36.2%)	154 (46.7%)
Numeral (indefinite determiner)	20 (4.8%)	100 (30.3%)
Total	414 (100.0%)	330 (100.0%)

Chi-square test $p<0.000$

The presence of overt indefinite determiners in Lamas can be accurately related to the dropping of the accusative marking. The data showed that, out of the 100 DPs with indefinite determiners, 88 (88.0%) of them did not have the accusative marker *-ta*. In the case of demonstratives, dropping occurred in 85 out of 154 (55.2%) instances. With bare nouns dropping was low in frequency, only 15 out of 76 (19.7%).

In Ulcumayo, on the other hand, definiteness did not correspond to the dropping of *-ta*. For all DP types (without determiner, with a demonstrative or with a numeral) *-ta* was more frequent than dropping. These facts favor the view that *-ta* has some determiner-like properties as proposed in Chapter 2 such as the licensing of null nouns, a property also shared by Spanish determiners

---

11. In the narratives the referents were either definite or specific and the likelihood of producing a generic DP was very low.

but that cannot be identified with definiteness or specificity.[12] The co-occurrence of the dropping of *-ta* in Lamista Quechua with a more extended use of indefinite and definite determiners indicates that in this variety, a new overt determiner system is emerging that replaces *-ta* in its determiner-like functions. In this case, the prediction of the Functional Convergence Hypothesis is borne given that the set of features related to definiteness and specificity does not have a morphological correlate in Quechua nor does it seem to be crucial in determining syntactic relationships. However, in Spanish such features are crucial in determining differences in the distribution and interpretation of direct objects and pronominal forms.[13] In this particular case, activation of those features in Spanish results in convergence in Quechua on a specific set of features assigned to the overt functional category D. Apparently, the bilingual Quechua object system is one in which D, null or overt, is specified for ± specific, ±definite features.

4.1.3.2 *Distribution of (S)OV/VO structures*

Overt DPs were categorized according to their position in the sentence. For sentences with overt subjects, the most frequent word order was SVO in both groups, as shown in Table 12.

---

12. Contreras (1989), Bernstein (1994), Martin (1996) and Sanchez (1996) among others discuss these cases for Spanish.

13. In Standard Spanish direct objects with null determiners are restricted to generic NPs of the type:

(i) María compra zapatos
    'Maria buys shoes'

Table 12. Distribution of sentential word order

Word order	Ulcumayo	Lamas
S V O	211 (29.6%)	262 (51.2%)
S O V	71 (9.9%)	29 (5.7%)
S (null obj)V (null obj)[14]	211 (29.6%)	151 (29.5%)
Pro subj V O	71 (9.9%)	25 (4.9%)
Pro subj O V	74 (10.4%)	7 (1.4%)
Pro subj V pro obj	60 (8.4%)	14 (2.7%)
O V S	6 (0.8%)	12 (2.3%)
O S V	4 (0.6%)	3 (0.6%)
V S O	2 (0.3%)	3 (0.6%)
V O S	1 (0.1%)	1 (0.2%)
V pro obj S	3 (0.4%)	5 (1.0%)
Total	714 (100.0%)	512 (100.0%)

Chi-square test $p<0.000$

These results go against the traditional characterization of all Quechua varieties as having an SOV canonical word order. However, it is not surprising, if we consider the significance of Spanish having an SVO canonical word order and the syntactic analysis provided for that order in Chapter 2. It is worth noting that the SVO word order has a higher frequency of occurrence in Lamas than in Ulcumayo. While in Lamas SVO reaches 51.2%, in Ulcumayo it reaches only 29.6%. The following are examples of SVO sentences from an Ulcumayo and a Lamas narrative:

Ulcumayo (Participant U1)
(32) Tortuga mira-ya-n   algu-s   wambra.
      turtle   look-DUR-3SG dog-FOC boy
      'The turtle is looking at the dog (and) the boy'

Lamas (Participant L2)
(33) Suk wambriyu api-yka-n   suk papel-ta.
      a   boy   grab-DUR-3SG a   paper-ACC
      'A boy grabs a piece of paper'

---

14. It would be very difficult to hypothesize about the position of the null object in this type of sentences. For that reason the null object has been located in either pre-verbal or post-verbal position in this informal representation.

Notice also that canonical SOV word order is not completely absent from the narratives from the two groups but there are no marked differences in its frequency in the narratives (9.9% in Ulcumayo and 5.7% in Lamas). The following are examples of canonical SOV word order:

Lamas (Participant L5)
(34) Suk motelo saputa   kawa-yka-n.
     a   turtle   Toad-ACC see-DUR-3P
     'A turtle sees a toad'

Ulcumayo (Participant U23)
(35) Wambra-m saputa   chari-ya.
     boy-FOC   toad-ACC hold-DUR
     'The boy is holding the toad'

According to the syntactic analysis presented in Chapter 2, the high frequency of SVO word order in Quechua can be analyzed as evidence of the projection of a ClP in the bilingual Quechua grammar. Canonical SVO word order is a major syntactic change in the grammar of Quechua and is predicted by the Functional Interference Hypothesis. It is triggered by the constant activation of the Cl features that require verb movement to Cl in Spanish.

Indeed one could argue that the bilingual grammars of Ulcumayo and Lamas Quechua are in the process of converging towards the feature specification for ClP in Spanish as predicted by the Functional Convergence Hypothesis. The verb moves to Cl and the overt subject moves to Spec of ClP. Such a process appears to be more generalized in the Lamas Quechua narratives than in the Ulcumayo ones. I interpret the coexistence of SVO and SOV word orders as implying that two competing strategies for canonical word order are available in Bilingual Quechua, particularly in Ulcumayo Quechua: one in which SOV represented without ClP projection and another one in which SVO is represented with a ClP projection. However, constant activation of the Spanish features for Cl will in the long run result in a similar frequency of convergence such as the one found in Lamas.

The second most frequent word order configuration for both groups were sentences with overt pre-verbal subjects and null objects. This order had nearly identical proportions in the two corpora, 29.6% in Ulcumayo and 29.5% in Lamas. The following sentence exemplifying this order immediately followed sentence (35) in the speech of Participant U23 and it refers to Figure 3 (see Appendix I) in which the turtle is clearly looking at the small toad:

Ulcumayo (Participant U23)
(36) Tortuga # rishka-ya pro.
 turtle look-DUR pro
 'The turtle is looking (at him)'

This word order shows evidence of a clear preference in the Quechua narratives for null objects with definite or specific antecedents.

In null subject sentences with overt objects, both object positions are more frequent in Ulcumayo than in Lamas, with a slight preference for OV in Ulcumayo versus a slight preference for VO in Lamas. The following examples illustrate OV word order taken from the Ulcumayo data (37) and VO from the Lamas data (38):

OV. Ulcumayo (Participant U18)
(37) Palu-ta apa-ya-n.
 stick-ACC carry-DUR-3S
 '(He) carries a stick'

VO. Lamas (Participant L6)
(38) Abrasa-yka-n achk-ita-n-ta.
 hug-DUR-3SG dog-DIM-3SG-ACC
 '(He) is hugging his dog'

The number of VO sentences is low but the example in (38) could indicate a greater flexibility in the Lamas group to move the verb outside the VP than in the Ulcumayo group. Such flexibility may be better understood in light of similar results found in the Spanish narratives and discussed in Chapter 5.

With respect to null subjects and null objects, they both appeared more frequently in sentences in Ulcumayo than in Lamas. The following example illustrates this case. The sentence refers to Figure 3 (see Appendix I) in which the boy has the little toad in his hand and is letting it go on the floor.

(39) Chariyan.
 hold-DUR-3SG
 '(He) is holding (him)'

The remaining word orders were very infrequent; the data show a low frequency of fronted objects when the subject is present. This makes it very difficult to assess whether interference or convergence has taken place. Both OVS and OSV word orders are very low in frequency and it is difficult to tease out whether their main difference (movement versus base generation of O) has been the subject of interference by the opposite values in Spanish. Example (40) illustrates the case of a fronted object marked with the topic suffix -*ka*.

OVS Lamas (Participant L18)
(40) Ishkay sapitu-ta-ka   api-yka-n   kay wambriyo.
    two   toad-ACC-TOPIC hold-DUR-3SG this boy
    'The boy is holding two toads'

Example (41) illustrates the case of an OSV sentence that should be in principle base generated. Notice that in this sentence the direct object does not bear a topic marker:

OSV Ulcumayo (Participant U18)
(41) Agash-ta tortuga-ta carga-ya-n[15]
    toad-ACC turtle-DEF carry-DUR-3SG
    'The turtle is carrying the toad(s)'

Finally, there was a very low frequency of fronted verbs and most of them were Spanish verbs. In Ulcumayo VSO occurred only with Spanish verbs although in the two cases registered, the subject and the object were Quechua DPs. In Lamas, two of the VSO cases had a Quechua verb and one, a Spanish verb. The DPs were also Quechua. The VOS cases in Lamas and Ulcumayo also involved Spanish verbs. Perhaps a different type of task would make it possible to find evidence of interference in the features that trigger verb movement in verb-initial clauses in both languages.

To summarize, these data show evidence of a strong tendency to prefer SVO word order, particularly in Lamas. I have suggested that this syntactic change is the result of interference triggered by the constant activation of the functional features of Cl in Spanish. Evidence in favor of this proposal will be presented in Chapter 5. Such interference is leading to convergence in the set of features of Cl that results in SVO as the canonical word order shared by the two languages in the bilingual mind. Convergence in the specification of Cl does not necessarily preclude the existence of SOV word orders, which I have analyzed in Chapter 2 as involving movement of the direct object to the specifier of the lower VP and no verb movement. In fact, they may coexist for a while, since for some speakers different word orders may involve different functional projections.

---

15. This sentence refers to Figure 7 (see Appendix I) and in it the turtle is carrying two toads on his back. As in other cases, the subject appears marked with the suffix -*ta*, which rather than an accusative marker, seems to be a marker of definiteness.

At the same time, convergence towards the set of values related to Cl is clearly more frequent than towards the lack of verb movement in Quechua.

The data also show that, despite prolonged contact with Spanish, null objects with definite or specific referents are still part of the grammar of Bilingual Quechua in Ulcumayo and Lamas.

4.1.4 Distribution of direct objects and their antecedents in discourse

In order to better understand the role that their status as topics has on the distribution of direct object complements, an analysis of the frequency of their antecedents in discourse was conducted. If a DP introduces a new topic in discourse it is unlikely that it will have an antecedent in the narrative. If, on the other hand, a topic has already been introduced in discourse by a direct object DP, and given that the grammar of Quechua has no overt third person direct object agreement or unfocused overt pronouns, then one expects that the null pronoun will be used to refer to this previous antecedent. In that respect, antecedents are used as cues to determine whether an overt DP or a null pronominal are required in discourse. I would like to argue that this type of distribution in discourse acts as a very strong cue in favor of convergence towards adopting specificity and definiteness values for D features in Spanish. In this subsection, I will present the distribution of antecedents in the Quechua narratives and I will refer back to it in the next chapter.

In coding the narratives, the term antecedent was used to label the character or element in the pictures or in discourse that was the referent for the direct object. Sentence (42) has an overt DP *achku-n-ta* 'his dog' in direct object position. Participant L8 had not previously mentioned it, and it clearly refers to the dog in Figure 16 (see Appendix I):

Lamas (Participant L8)
(42) Kay wambriyu # markaykan achku-n-ta.
    this boy   cradles   dog-3SG-ACC
    'This boy cradles his dog'

In this case, the direct object was coded as having an antecedent not present in the text but identifiable.

Antecedents previously mentioned in the text were coded according to their syntactic or morphological representations. They could be full DPs in Quechua or in Spanish, complex DPs, demonstrative pronouns, strong or null pronouns.

The following examples from an Ulcumayo narrative illustrate the case of a DP antecedent for a null pronoun:

Ulcumayo (Participant U25)
(43) Niño chiriyan saputa$_i$.
 the boy grab-3SG toad-ACC$_i$
 'The boy grabs the toad'

(44) Algok mira-ya-n pro$_i$.
 dog look-DURA-3SG pro$_i$
 'The dog looks at him'

In sentence (44) the null pronoun has the direct object DP *saputa* in (43) as its antecedent. The co-indexing is clearly disambiguated by the picture that the child is describing (Figure 3 in Appendix I). In general, given the fixed number of animate and inanimate characters in the pictures, there was a limited set of potential antecedents in the discourse. Antecedents were traced back to their immediately previous mention. For both groups, I found that the most frequent direct object antecedent was an overt DP, 56.9% of the cases for Ulcumayo and 60.3% for Lamas. That is, DPs are the linguistic expressions that serve most frequently the function of anchoring a referent as discussed in Abney (1986) and Longobardi (1994). A DP may serve as the antecedent of a null pronoun as exemplified in (44) or as the antecedent of a full DP. The following excerpt exemplifies the latter cases:

Ulcumayo (Participant U4)
(45) Kaychuga # **agash ichikllalla-ta** hati-ru-n chiwchiga, algu-ga
 then toad little-ACC take out-PAST-3SG boy dog-TOP
 gallun hitasha #
 tongue-3SG stick out
 'Then the boy took out the little toad, the dog sticking out his tongue'

(46) pro risga-ra-ya-n **agaslla-ta-ga.**
 pro look-PAST-DUR-3SG toad-ACC-TOP
 '(He) was looking at the toad'

In sentence (45), the DP *agash ichikllalata* 'the little toad' has already been introduced in the discourse as the direct object of an action accomplished by the boy. A change of discourse topic takes place when the child refers to a new agent (the dog) performing a newly introduced action (sticking out his tongue). As the narrative continues, the dog remains the main topic of discourse but the little toad needs to be reintroduced in discourse. In these cases, a DP is used to recover old information previously introduced and therefore a DP has as its antecedent another DP. Notice that this is precisely the type of context in which a clitic doubling expression would be used in many varieties of Latin American Spanish, as noted in Chapter 2.

The second most common antecedent for the Ulcumayo group was the null pronoun. The following fragment illustrates the case in which a null pronoun serves as an antecedent for an overt DP. In (48) the DP *algu-ga* 'the dog-topic' is introduced in this fragment of discourse. It is the antecedent of the null pronoun in (49). In (50) and (51) new discourse topics are introduced as the subjects of these sentences (*tortuga* 'turtle' and *sapu* 'toad'). Then a question by the interviewer recovers 'the boy' as the subject of discourse in (52) and in (53) 'the dog' reappears as the object of the action of being hugged. It reappears as a full DP with the null pronoun as its closest antecedent in (49).

Ulcumayo (Participant U24)

(47) *CHI: Niñu-ga tara-ya.
boy-TOP sit-DUR
'The boy is sitting'

(48) Chaypita **alguga**$_i$ # marga-man ni-ya-n.
then dog$_i$ # cradle-COND say-DUR-3SG
'Then (he) cradles the dog, (he) says'

(49) Chaypi niñuga marga-ya-n **pro**$_j$.
then boy-TOP cradle-DUR-3SG pro$_i$
'The boy is cradling (him)'

(50) Chaypi tortuga chaychu # tirara-ya-n.
then turtle then # sit-DUR-3SG
'Then the turtle is sitting'

(51) Chaypita sapu chaychu tara-ya-n.
then toad then sit-DUR-3SG
'Then the toad is sitting'

(52) *INT: ¿Imata rura-ya-n wambra?
what do-DUR-3SG boy
'What is the boy doing?'

(53) *CHI: **Algu-ta**$_i$ marga-ra-ya-n.
dog-ACC craddle-PAST-DUR-3SG
'(He) was cradling the dog'

This indicates that at least for the Ulcumayo data null pronouns are used to express immediate topics in discourse while overt DPs are used to introduce or reintroduce them.

For the Lamas group, the second most frequent antecedent was the antecedent not mentioned in the text (24% compared with 14.9% in the Ulcumayo data). For this type of antecedent, the speakers relied heavily on the knowledge shared by the interlocutor, since the interviewers and the participants looked at the same set of pictures together. Example (42) from Lamas illustrates how this type of antecedent works. Table 13 compares the differences in frequencies of direct object antecedents for the two groups.

Table 13. Types of direct object antecedents in the narratives

Antecedents	Ulcumayo	Lamas
DP (Q)	327 (46.1%)	284 (55.8%)
DP (S)	77 (10.8%)	23 (4.5%)
Complex DP (Q)	1 (0.1%)	3 (0.6%)
Null	186 (26.2%)	70 (13.8%)
Not mentioned in the text	106 (14.9%)	122 (24.0%)
Not identifiable	4 (0.6%)	5 (1.0%)
Strong pronoun (Q)	3 (0.4%)	1 (0.2%)
Demonstrative pronoun (Q,S)	6 (0.8%)	1 (0.2%)
Total	710 (100.0%)	509 (100.0%)

Chi-square test $p<0.0000$

As stated above, DPs were more frequent antecedents, probably because of the nature of the task and the type of discourse it elicited. Null pronoun antecedents were almost twice as frequent in Ulcumayo than in Lamas. This high frequency in the Quechua narratives will be compared in the next chapter to the frequency of null object antecedents in the Spanish narratives. Antecedents not mentioned in the text were more frequent in the narratives from Lamas confirming a tendency to use DPs and pronouns deictically.[16] Strong pronouns and demonstrative pronouns were very infrequent as antecedents for other direct object constructions (less than 1%).

---

16. This tendency, in the use of null pronouns was already observed in an article reporting on the results of the pilot for this study (Sanchez 2002).

4.1.5 Distribution of direct object complements according to their antecedents

With respect to the types of antecedents that the direct objects have in the narratives, Table 14 shows that DPs had as their most common antecedents other DPs. This indicates a tendency to repeat them, as if the topics were to be reintroduced constantly. For the Ulcumayo group, null object antecedents were the second most frequent type. This indicates that in the Ulcumayo narratives a null pronominal behaves as a topic throughout discourse. The percentage for null object antecedents was lower in Lamas. On the other hand, the frequency for antecedents not present in the text was higher for the DPs in Lamas than in Ulcumayo. I take this to indicate that the children in Lamas used more deictic clues than the children in Ulcumayo to establish their discourse referents.

Table 14. DP (Q and S) structures according to their antecedents

Antecedent	Ulcumayo	Lamas
DP(Q, S)	260 (66.0%)	200 (65.6%)
Null	72 (18.3%)	34 (11.1%)
Not in the text	57 (14.5%)	65 (21.3%)
Other[a]	5 (1.3%)	6 (2.0%)
Total	394 (100.0%)	305 (100.0%)

[a] Includes unidentifiable, strong pronoun, demonstrative pronoun Quechua and Spanish, clitic and clitic doubling. No cases of complex antecedent.
Chi-square test $p < 0.0122$

I also analyzed the definiteness and specificity of antecedents. The results are shown in Table 15. In the case of Quechua DPs it was clear that the Ulcumayo data patterned more clearly with the grammatical descriptions of Quechua. The data show a higher percentage of DPs not marked for definiteness that can be interpreted as specific in the context. The Lamas data, on the other hand, have a significantly higher frequency of definite and indefinite specific antecedents in Quechua, which indicates a tendency to pattern with Spanish in requiring overt definite or indefinite determiners. Notice that such a tendency is maintained throughout discourse and that it serves the purpose of linking DPs in discourse.

Null objects are of particular importance to the two hypotheses proposed in this book. In order to explain their pervasiveness in Bilingual Spanish varieties in terms of interference or convergence with the Quechua null objects, it was

Table 15. Definiteness and specificity of an antecedent (Quechua DP)

Antecedent	Lamas		Ulcumayo	
Definite specific	139	(48.9%)	88	(27.1%)
Indefinite specific	123	(43.3%)	53	(16.3%)
Unmarked for definiteness or specificity	22	(7.7%)	184	(56.6%)
Total	284 (100.0%)		325 (100.0%)	

Chi-square test $p<0.0000$

Table 16. Null objects according to their antecedents

Antecedent	Ulcumayo		Lamas	
DP(Q)	104	(38.1%)	97	(56.1%)
DP(S)	23	(8.4%)	7	(4.0%)
Not in the text	31	(11.4%)	29	(16.8%)
Null	109	(39.9%)	34	(19.7%)
Other[a]	6	(2.2%)	6	(3.5%)
Total	273 (100.0%)		173 (100.0%)	

[a] Includes complex antecedents, unidentifiable antecedents, Quechua strong pronouns, and demonstrative pronouns.
Chi-square test $p<0.000018$

necessary to observe their distribution in Quechua discourse. Table 16 shows their distribution according to antecedent.

One of the main differences between the narratives from Ulcumayo and Lamas is the higher frequency of DPs (Quechua and Spanish) as antecedents for null pronouns in Lamas. In contrast, null objects were more frequent as antecedents for other null pronouns in the Ulcumayo narratives. The following examples illustrate this latter case. They refer to Figure 3 where the boy is holding the little toad, and the big toad, the turtle and the dog are looking at the little toad:

(54) CHI: Wambracha chari-ya-n **sapu-ta$_i$**.
 boy hold-DUR-3SG toad-ACC$_i$
 'The boy is holding the toad'

(55) INT: Chaypitaga?
 'And then?'

(56) CHI: Sapuchas mira-ya-n **pro$_j$**.
 toad-DIM look-DUR-3SG pro$_j$
 'The toad is looking (at him)'

(57) INT: Chaypitaga alinmi.
'And then, good'

(58) Chaypitaga?
'And then?'

(59) CHI: Tortugacha rirga-ya-n   pro$_j$.
turtle   look-DUR-3SG pro$_j$
'The turtle is looking at him'

It would seem that, in both varieties of Quechua, the null pronoun in object position is identified throughout discourse as the topic even when the subject DPs are changed. However, in the narratives in Ulcumayo Quechua, there was a higher frequency in the use of such discourse identification as a narrative strategy. If this strategy is prevalent in the Quechua grammar one expects that it reinforce the use of null pronouns in Spanish with the same discourse functions irrespectively of the specificity or definiteness of the antecedents.

To summarize, in this chapter I have shown evidence from the Quechua narratives in favor of interference in functional features. Both bilingual groups had similar low frequencies of Spanish verbal and noun roots. At the same time, the data showed a high frequency of SVO word order configurations, particularly in Lamas. I have suggested that this is evidence of a syntactic change in Quechua driven by interference in the feature specifications of the Spanish functional projection Cl that requires verb movement to Cl and subject movement to spec of ClP. This interference is leading to convergence in the specification of Cl in canonical sentences in Spanish and in Quechua. The Spanish data discussed in Chapter 5 will provide evidence of the constant activation of clitics that, I will argue, favors the projection of ClP in Quechua. Thus, the Quechua data in conjunction with the Spanish data that I will discuss in the next chapter confirm the predictions that the Functional Convergence Hypothesis makes according to which the constant activation of functional features present only in one of the languages represented in the bilingual mind may result in the emergence of a functional category in the other language.

The narratives from Lamas also showed a higher frequency of dropping of the accusative suffix -*ta* in overt DPs than those from Ulcumayo. Accusative dropping in the Lamas narratives co-occurred with an increased use of overt demonstratives and indefinite determiners. This is evidence of convergence favoring the Spanish feature specification of D that privileges overt determiners in overt DPs.

Three categories had very low frequencies of occurrence as direct object complements. These were overt strong pronouns, demonstrative pronouns and CP structures. This low frequency can be attributed to the nature of the task. There were some instances of Spanish clitics. These were present mostly in VPs with Spanish verbs and in the narratives of children who favored intra-sentential code-mixing. The use of clitics is indicative of the activation of Cl features.

Finally, the analysis of antecedents showed that in discourse the two most frequent antecedents for both groups were overt DPs and null pronouns. I proposed that Quechua null objects are identified as topics in discourse, and may serve as antecedents to other null pronouns. This discourse strategy seemed to be less favored by the Lamas group than by the Ulcumayo group. This type of discourse strategy will become relevant to account for the pervasiveness of null objects with definite antecedents in bilingual Spanish in the next chapter.

CHAPTER 5

The frog is looking at Phi-features
Functional convergence in bilingual Spanish

In this chapter, I will present the results of the story-telling task and of the picture-sentence-matching task in Spanish. I will focus on those data that indicate differences between the bilingual groups from Ulcumayo and Lamas and the "monolingual" group from San Juan with respect to the representation of the Spanish grammar. I will propose that they are evidence of syntactic changes that result from functional interference and are also evidence of functional convergence triggered by constant activation of features.

As mentioned in Chapter 4, the story-telling task had as its main goal the elicitation of transitive verbs and direct object complements. As in the case of the Quechua narratives, an analysis of the distribution of direct objects was undertaken in order to find evidence of interference and convergence in the feature specification of functional categories such as Cl and D. The analysis of the distribution of overt DPs, clitics and null direct objects aimed at providing evidence in favor of interference or convergence in phi-features such as definiteness, gender and number features in Cl and D, especially since Spanish, unlike Quechua, has a phonologically overt clitic system that encodes those phi-features and lacks null objects with definite antecedents. It was expected that interference from Quechua would allow the licensing of null object pronouns with definite antecedents, especially, if bilinguals used the same discourse strategies for topic recovery in Spanish and Quechua.

The data from the story-telling task provides some evidence in favor of convergence in the functional features associated with null pronouns. There was a higher frequency of null objects used to refer to definite antecedents and antecedents not present in the text in the bilingual data than in the monolingual data. There was also strong evidence of convergence in the feature specification of clitics in the form of neutralization of gender and case differences in the clitic system of the bilinguals. Unlike in the Quechua narratives, there were no instances of code-switching to Quechua and very few cases of verbal lexical borrowings from Quechua were found (2 lexical items in Ulcumayo and 2 in Lamas).

The picture-sentence matching task did not show clear results for the bilinguals. It showed some distinct tendencies among the monolinguals to prefer overt clitics over null pronouns, and clitic doubling structures over strong pronouns.

This chapter is divided in two main subsections. In the first one, the results of the story-telling task are presented. A similar distribution of the verbal lexical items in the Spanish narratives for three groups shows low levels of lexical interference from Quechua in verbal roots. A discussion of the distribution of direct object complements ensues that focuses on evidence for functional interference and convergence in phi-features and draws comparisons with the data from the bilingual Quechua narratives. Finally, an analysis of direct object antecedents is presented that supports the notion that similar discourse strategies are used by bilinguals to select from a set of possible pronominal forms to continue or re-introduce topics in discourse. The last sub-section of the chapter presents the results of the picture-sentence matching task and relates them to the findings in the story-telling task.

5.1 Story-telling task results in bilingual Spanish

At first sight, the data from the story-telling task in Spanish showed an apparent similarity in the distribution of the direct object structures in the narratives of the three groups studied. However, a more detailed analysis of the antecedents for the direct object structures shows that there are some important differences among groups in terms of the discourse restrictions imposed on the selection of direct object pronominals. The type of direct object structures typically found in Standard Spanish that I expected to find in the data were: full DPs,[1] direct object clitic pronouns, demonstrative pronouns, clitic left dislocation structures (CLLD), clitic doubling structures and complementizer phrase (CP) complements. Given the findings of previous studies on bilingual varieties of Spanish in contact with Quechua (Escobar, A.M. 1994a, Paredes 1997, Camacho, Paredes and Sanchez 1996, Sanchez 1998 and Sanchez 2002), I expected to find in the bilingual narratives cases of null objects with definite antecedents and perhaps clitic doubling with indefinites and CP complements. These structures,

---

1. The category DP includes fronted DPs that may correspond to either topicalized or focalized structures. The data on fronted versus non-fronted DPs is presented later in this chapter.

if present at all in the "monolingual" narratives from San Juan de Miraflores, were expected to be low in frequency. In the following sub-sections, I present the results.

5.1.1 Consistency in the type of verbs used by the children in the narratives

The story-telling task showed a similar average of verbs per child for the two bilingual groups. The bilinguals produced a high number of verb tokens; for the group in Lamas (the group with access to bilingual education) it was 23.9% and for the bilingual group in Ulcumayo it was 24%. This is shown in Table 1. For the monolingual group the average was lower, 17.8%, which indicates that bilinguals produced a higher number of verb tokens. In general, variation was greater among bilinguals than among monolinguals, as shown by the standard deviation which was 8.64 for the monolingual children in San Juan, 10.88 for the bilingual children in Lamas and even greater in Ulcumayo, 11.20. The patterns of maximum and minimum number of verbs for each group did not differ greatly, indicating a similar composition in terms of the most and least productive narratives. The differences in variation were minor and they allow for a comparison of the results for the three groups.

Table 1. Verbs in Spanish narratives

	San Juan de Miraflores ("monolingual" group)	Lamas	Ulcumayo
Average	17.8	23.9	24.0
SD	8.64	10.88	11.20
Max	44	54	48
Min	6	6	4
Number of verbs	639	717	672
Number of children	36	30	28

The ratio of verb tokens/verb types for the three groups did not differ significantly, as shown in Table 2.

As in the case of the Quechua narratives, there was greater variation in verb types when the number of tokens was low. As the number of tokens per verb type increases, there is greater similarity in the use of verb types. The distribution of verb types and tokens according to lexical items for each group are shown in Appendix IV. The most frequent verb types for the three groups were *ver* 'see', *mirar* 'look', *agarrar* 'catch' and *botar* 'throw'. Although the number of

Table 2. Distribution of tokens and types of verbs according to group

	San Juan de Miraflores	Lamas	Ulcumayo	Total
Token	717	639	672	2028
Type	68	78	66	124
Variability	0.09	0.12	0.10	0.06

tokens for these verb types differs for each group, they all have more than 15 tokens. In other words, there is less semantic variation among groups in verbs used most frequently. This indicates that there is a core set of verbs in the narratives for which the three groups showed a somewhat similar pattern of verb selection. Thus, the differences in distribution of direct object complements should not be attributed to different patterns of verb use among the groups. As for the comparison with verb types in Quechua, the Ulcumayo group produced fewer verb types in Spanish than in Quechua and the Lamas groups produced more verb types in Spanish than in Quechua (see Chapter 4).

5.1.2 Distribution of direct object complements in Spanish narratives: Clitic and D features as evidence of interference and convergence

As in the case of the Quechua narratives, an analysis of the distribution of direct object complements was carried out. Each transitive verb token and its direct object complement were coded. There was an apparent similarity among the three groups in the ordering of structures according to frequency. However, the results of the chi-square test applied to the data for the three groups show that there is a significant difference in the distribution of the direct objects as shown in Table 3.

As in the case of the Quechua narratives, for all groups, the most frequent type of direct object complement was an overt DP although it occurred slightly less frequently in the monolingual data (33.8%) than in the bilingual data (Lamas 35.4% and Ulcumayo 39.7%).[2] The following examples from the monolingual and bilingual groups illustrate these cases:

---

2. These numbers include post-verbal and pre-verbal overt DPs, but they exclude clitic left dislocations and clitic doubling structures.

Table 3. Distribution of direct object complements

Transitive verb complement	San Juan de Miraflores		Lamas		Ulcumayo	
DP (Determiner Phrase)	216	(33.8%)	254	(35.4%)	267	(39.7%)
Clitic	197	(30.8%)	180	(25.1%)	177	(26.3%)
Clitic doubling (w/DP)	168	(26.3%)	182	(25.4%)	124	(18.5%)
Clitic Left Dislocation	16	(2.5%)	44	(6.1%)	35	(5.2%)
Null	10	(1.6%)	37	(5.2%)	45	(6.7%)
Duplicated clitic[3]	0	(0.0%)	1	(0.1%)	6	(0.9%)
Clitic doubling (w/strong pronoun, demonstrative)	1	(0.2%)	4	(0.6%)	11	(1.6%)
Strong Pronoun	0	(0.0%)	4	(0.6%)	0	(0.0%)
Demonstrative Pronoun	2	(0.3%)	1	(0.1%)	3	(0.4%)
CP (Complement Phrase)	26	(4.1%)	10	(1.4%)	4	(0.6%)
Doubled CP	3	(0.5%)	0	(0.0%)	0	(0.0%)
Total	639	(100.0%)	717	(100.0%)	672	(100.0%)

Chi-square test San Juan de Miraflores (SJM), Lamas (L), Ulcumayo (U) $p<0.000000$
Chi-square test (without clitic doubled CP) L, U $p<0.001947$

San Juan de Miraflores (Participant SJ32)
(1) Después el niño sacó un sapo.
    then the boy took out a toad
    'Then the boy took out a toad'

Lamas (Participant L12)
(2) Y este wamrillu está (a)gar(r)ando ese sap-ito.
    and this boy is holding this toad-DIM
    'And this boy is holding this little toad'

Ulcumayo (Participant U2)
(3) Acá el niño e(s)tá sacando el sapo de la caja.
    here the boy is taking the toad out of the box
    'Here the boy is taking the toad out of the box'

Direct object clitics were the second most frequent direct object. Again, they appeared slightly more frequently in the monolingual data (30.8%) than in the

---

3. These were cases in which a clitic appeared twice as in:
(i) Lo quiere verlo.
    Cl wants (to) see Cl
    '(S/he) want to see (him)'

bilingual data (Lamas 25.1% and Ulcumayo 26.3%) and were almost identical in frequency to the clitic doubling with a DP in the Lamas bilingual data. This indicates that clitics are part of the bilingual Spanish grammar, despite the fact that the Quechua narratives did not show evidence of clitics as part of the bilingual Quechua grammar.[4] The following sentences are examples with clitics from each of the groups:

San Juan de Miraflores (Participant SJ35)
(4) Y no lo encuentran.
 and not Cl find
 'And (they) don't find it'

Lamas (Participant L13)
(5) Y el perro le mira también.
 and the dog Cl looks too
 'And the dog looks at him too'

Ulcumayo (Participant U8)
(6) La tortuga le está mirando.
 the turtle Cl is looking
 'The turtle is looking at him'

In order to determine that there is a productive use of clitics in the Spanish narratives of the bilinguals, I checked for their use with different types of verbs in the three groups. The monolingual group in San Juan and the bilingual group in Lamas showed greater variation in verb types used with clitics than the Ulcumayo group. The latter showed a strong association of clitics with the verb *mirar* 'to look' but this conforms to the high frequency of use of this verb type in the Ulcumayo narratives (see Appendix IV). In general, clitics were used productively across verb types.

Thus, clitics are productive in these bilinguals. However, interference has produced changes in their Spanish morphosyntax, in particular when their data is compared to that of the "monolingual" group. Table 5 shows the contrasts in the distribution of the clitic forms across groups:

Whereas the morpheme *lo* (the accusative masculine singular clitic in Standard Spanish) was more frequent than *le* (the dative singular clitic with no gender specification) among monolinguals as a direct object clitic (see example 4), it was significantly less frequent among bilinguals. Both bilingual groups

---

4. They only appeared in code-mixing instances.

Table 4. Distribution of most frequent verbs with clitics

Verbs	San Juan de Miraflores		Lamas		Ulcumayo	
Mirar	36	(18.27%)	29	(16.11%)	83	(46.89%)
Botar	30	(15.23%)	7	(3.89%)	14	(7.91%)
Ver	15	(7.61%)	30	(16.67%)	6	(3.39%)
Morder	13	(6.60%)	22	(12.22%)	1	(0.56%)
Buscar	12	(6.09%)	1	(0.56%)	0	(0.00%)
Agarrar	4	(2.03%)	17	(9.44%)	15	(8.47%)
Seguir	3	(1.52%)	12	(6.67%)	9	(5.08%)
Other	84	(42.64%)	62	(34.44%)	49	(27.68%)
Total	197	(100.00%)	180	(100.00%)	177	(100.00%)

Chi test SJM, L, U $p<0.0000$
Chi test L, U $p<0.0000$

Table 5. Clitics forms

Clitics	San Juan de Miraflores		Lamas		Ulcumayo	
Lo	107	(54.3%)	43	(23.9%)	20	(11.3%)
La	21	(10.7%)	5	(2.8%)	14	(7.9%)
Le	66	(33.5%)	132	(73.3%)	143	(80.8%)
Los	2	(1.0%)	0	(0.0%)	0	(0.0%)
Les	1	(0.5%)	0	(0.0%)	0	(0.0%)
Total	197	(100.0%)	180	(100.0%)	177	(100.0%)

SJM, L, U $p<0.000000$
L, U $p<0.001448$

exhibited a strong preference for the form *le* as a direct object pronoun. This was not expected, at least for the Ulcumayo data, since in previous work on Spanish in contact with Quechua (see Escobar, A. M. 1990 and Escobar, A. 1978 among others) in the Andean regions no particular preference for *le* forms is attested as a characteristic of bilingual Andean Spanish. Examples (4), (5) and (6) show these contrasts.

The clitic *la* (accusative feminine singular) was also infrequent for all groups. This could be due to the way the instrument was constructed (see Chapter 3 and Appendix I); only two objects depicted in the pictures could have elicited the clitic *la*. These were a box and a turtle (in Spanish *la caja* 'the box' and *la tortuga* 'a turtle').[5] However infrequent, *la* did appear in some bilingual

---

5. For the bilingual group in Lamas, the feminine form 'la' was even less frequent because the

narratives, which shows that it is not completely absent from the input the children receive. Despite this presence, mismatches between the gender specification of the clitic and its antecedent were found. The following examples from San Juan illustrate the type of matching in gender between an antecedent marked for feminine and the feminine clitic *la*:

> San Juan (Participant SJ 29)
>
> (7) Después el niño ha cargado la ranita
> then the boy has picked up the froggy
> 'Then the boy picked up the froggy'
>
> (8) y la puso en la cabecita del # perro.
> and Cl put on the head of-the # dog
> and put her on the frog's head

The following fragment from an Ulcumayo narrative illustrates a case in which the closest antecedent in discourse for the feminine clitic *la* is a masculine NP.

> Ulcumayo (Participant U7)
>
> (9) *CHI: Acá el niño se asustó
> here the boy Cl-REFL frightened
> 'Here the boy got frightned'
>
> (10) *CHI: porque al sapo$_i$ le$_i$ pegó.
> because to the toad$_i$ Cl-DAT$_i$ hit
> 'because (he) hit the toad'
>
> (11) *INT: ¿Quién?
> 'Who?'
>
> (12) *CHI: El otro sapo$_j$.
> 'The other toad$_j$'
>
> (13) *INT: Uhum #.
>
> (14) *CHI: Acá uno con su xxx le$_i$ está agarró.
> here one with his xxx Cl-DAT$_i$ is grabbing
> 'Here one with his xxx is grabbing it'
>
> (15) *CHI: Los demás mirando para allá.
> the others looking for there
> 'The others looking there'

---

alternative masculine noun *el motelo* was used to refer to the turtle, thus the percentage of feminine clitics is even lower.

(16) *INT: Uhum #.
(17) *CHI: Y el perro la$_j$ quiere comer.
         and the dog   Cl-FEM$_j$ wants eat
         'And the dog want to eat her'

In this fragment, sentence (10) introduces one of the toads that is being hit by another toad, in sentence (12) there is reference to this other toad *el otro sapo* 'the other toad' that is the agent of the action. Sentence (15) introduces a different subject and when 'the other toad' is recovered in (17) as the topic of discourse the child uses the feminine clitic *la* (see Figures 5 and 6 in Appendix I).

Given that Quechua lacks gender specifications for object agreement morphemes, mismatches in gender between the clitic and its antecedents as well as the strong preference for the dative form, which is unmarked for gender in Spanish, are indications of interference and convergence in the morphological features of the clitic. Notice that this preference is the counterpart to the preference for SVO word orders found in the bilingual Quechua narratives. A process of convergence in the features associated with the ClP projection is taking place in these bilingual populations such that it affects the gender specification of the clitic that checks these features in the head of ClP in bilingual Spanish and at the same time affects canonical word order in Quechua.

After DPs and clitics, clitic doubling structures were the third structure in frequency for the three groups. It was minimally higher than clitics in the Lamas narratives (see Table 3). As in the case of clitics, the *le* form was more frequent among bilinguals (79.1% in Lamas, 91.1% in Ulcumayo and 47.6% in San Juan). The following examples from the three groups illustrate cases of clitic doubling structures:

San Juan de Miraflores (Participant: SJ10)
(18)   El   perrito también lo   # cómo se   (ll)ama # lo$_i$ quería
       the doggy also   Cl$_{ACC}$ # how Cl$_{REF}$ call # Cl$_{ACC_i}$ wanted
       morder al   sapo$_i$.⁶
       bite   to-the toad$_i$
       'The doggy also it, how do you say it, wanted to bite the toad'

---

6. The expression *como se llama* lit. 'how is it called' functions in Peruvian Spanish as a discourse tag.

Lamas (Participant L13)
(19) Acá el motelu le$_i$ carga a un sapo$_j$.
       here the turtle Cl$_{DAT i}$ carries to a toad$_j$
       'Here the turtle carries a toad'

Ulcumayo (Participant U13)
(20) Se   asustó   él porque l'$_i$ ha mata(d)o al   chiquito
      Cl$_{REFL}$ frightened he because Cl$_{DAT i}$ has killed   to the little
      sapo$_j$.
      toad$_j$
      'He got frightened because he has killed the little toad'

The high frequency of the *le* clitic form in clitic doubling structures among the bilinguals provides further support to the idea that interference results in convergence in the specification of the clitic features in the bilingual Spanish grammar. There were also some instances of clitic doubling with indefinites as shown in example (19) but the use of structures with overt DPs and non-doubled clitics shows that clitics are not an obligatory agreement marker in the grammar of these participants.

Although ranked similarly in order of frequency for the three groups, CLLD structures, null pronouns and CPs are categories in which monolinguals and bilinguals differ. The contrast is greater for null objects. Out of all the direct object structures used in the narratives, null objects reached 6.7% in the narratives of the bilingual children in Ulcumayo and 5.2% in the narratives in Lamas while they only reached 1.6% in the narratives of the monolingual children. These are not high numbers, especially since, unlike the Quechua narratives, these data include clitic structures in them, but the difference between the "monolingual" group and the bilingual groups can be taken as an indication of some level of convergence on the features associated with null pronouns as topics throughout discourse. Such a difference will be further confirmed by the different results in the picture–sentence matching task obtained for the "monolingual" and the bilingual groups with respect to the preference for clitics over null objects.[7] The following examples illustrate instances of null objects with definite antecedents in the narratives of the three groups.[8]

---

7. These results are in line with the findings in previous works by Camacho, Paredes and Sanchez (1998), Camacho (1999), Sanchez (1998) and Sanchez (2002).

8. In all cases the antecedent can be clearly distinguished by looking at the figures, but is not expressed.

San Juan de Miraflores (Participant SJ8)

(21) Y   estaban buscando   al   sapo pequeño$_i$.
     and were   looking for the toad little$_i$
     'And (they) were looking for the little toad'

(22) La   tortuga estaba buscando   pro$_i$ en   un tronco vacío.
     the turtle   was   looking for pro$_i$ inside a   log   empty
     'The turtle was looking for it inside an empty log'

Lamas (Participant L28)

(23) ⟨Chay^9⟩ [//] ese   wamrillu$_i$ (e)stá metiendo su   mano en el
     ⟨that⟩   [//] that boy   is   putting   his hand in the
     cartón.
     cardboard (box)
     'That boy is putting his hand inside the box'

(24) Y   tortuga (e)stá mirando pro$_i$.
     and turtle   is   looking pro$_i$
     'And the turtle is looking at him'

Ulcumayo (Participant U9)

(25) Acá el   niño está agarra(d)o a   un sapito$_i$.
     here the boy is   holding   to a   toad$_i$
     'Here the boy is holding a toad'

(26) ⟨El   perrito⟩ [/] el   perrito está miró   pro$_i$.
     ⟨the doggy⟩   [/] the doggy is   looked pro$_i$
     'The doggy is looking at him'

CLLD structures were also less frequent in the narratives of monolinguals (2.5%) than in those of bilinguals (6.1% in Lamas and 5.2% in Ulcumayo). The following examples illustrate cases of CLLD constructions in the narratives of the three groups:

San Juan (Participant SJ34)

(27) Y   el   &sa y   al   sapo grande$_i$ pro lo$_i$ están dejando.
     and the f   and to-the frog big$_i$ pro Cl$_{ACC_i}$ are   leaving
     'And (they) are leaving the big frog'

---

9. The child uses the word *chay* 'this' in Quechua.

Lamas (Participant L25)
(28) A ese motelo$_i$ lo$_i$ está montando un sapo abierto su changa.
       to that turtle   ClACC$_i$ is   mounting a   frog open   his leg
       'A frog with his legs open is mounting that turtle'

Ulcumayo (Participant U26)
(29) A éste$_i$ le$_i$ mató.
       to this Cl$_i$ killed
       'He killed this one'

However low in frequency in this task, the presence of CLLD structures in the bilingual narratives confirms the projection of a ClP functional category in bilingual Spanish. In Chapter 4, I suggested that ClP was responsible for SVO canonical word orders in bilingual Quechua. Its presence in bilingual Spanish supports the idea that it is a projection common to both languages in the bilingual children.

In addition to clitic left dislocation structures, I also checked for possible instances of a fronted direct object without a clitic of the type found in Quechua. There were very few cases of OV word orders and a strong preference for VO word order. The frequency of OV word order was slightly higher for the two bilingual groups than for the monolingual group (see Table 6).

Table 6. DP (VO versus OV)

Verb position with DP complements	San Juan de Miraflores	Lamas	Ulcumayo
DP (VO)	214 (99.1%)	245 (96.5%)	255 (95.5%)
DP (OV)	2 (0.9%)	9 (3.5%)	12 (4.5%)
Total	216 (100%)	254 (100%)	267 (100%)

SJM, L, U $p<0.072152$
L, U $p<0.581147$

The following example from Ulcumayo illustrates cases of fronting without a clitic:

Ulcumayo (Participant: U26)
(30) Acá su sapo chiquito (es)tá agarrando.
       here his toad little   is   grabbing
       'Here (he) is grabbing his little toad'

Example (30) cannot be analyzed as a typical Spanish CLLD structure because it lacks the clitic and the preposition *a* required in Spanish. It could be interpreted either as a case of canonical OV word order with a null subject or as a topicalization with a null subject. Muysken (1984) has proposed that these cases are compatible with an analysis in which the fronted DP is in a topic position but no ClP is projected as in the Quechua OSV or OVS structures (see Chapter 2). Convergence in the feature specification of Topic Phrase in Spanish and Quechua would be at play in these limited cases. The coexistence of SVO word orders in Quechua and CLLD structures in Spanish indicates that there is convergence in ClP and, at the same time, there are some cases in which there is interference from Quechua in topic features that results in OV word orders in Spanish.

As for CP direct object complements, these were more frequent in the narratives of the monolingual group (4%) than they were in the narratives of the bilingual groups (1.4% in Lamas and 0.6% in Ulcumayo). The following are examples of CPs from each group:

San Juan de Miraflores (Participant SJ22)
(31) La ranita más grande prometió que pro nunca sentirá envidia
 the froggy more big promised that pro never feel envious
 (d)e los demás.
 of the others.
 'The bigger frog promised that (he) will never feel envious of others'

Lamas (Participant L 23)
(32) El motelu cree que está durmiendo viendo los ojos.
 the turtle thinks that is sleeping looking at the eyes
 'The turtle thinks that (he) is sleeping (because) he is looking at his eyes'

Ulcumayo (Participant U10)
(33) E(s)tá mirando lo que saca.
 is looking it that takes out
 '(He) is looking at what he takes out'

Again the numbers in this case are low and presumably the task did not lend itself to the production of such structures. However, example (33) is interesting because it shows a type of complement clause that involves some form of nominalization in Spanish expressed by the use of the pronoun *lo* preceding the CP. As mentioned in Chapter 2, complement clauses in Quechua are nominalizations.

Finally, very few instances of demonstrative pronouns were found in the narratives of the three groups, and strong pronouns were found only in the Lamas narratives. The following examples from the San Juan de Miraflores and the Lamas data illustrate cases of demonstrative pronouns found in the three groups and the case of a strong pronoun found in Lamas.

Demonstrative pronoun, San Juan de Miraflores (Participant SJ22)
(34) Y   como eso vio el   niño le   regañó muy fuerte.
      and as   that saw the boy Cl<small>DAT</small> told off very strongly
      'And as (he) saw that the boy told him off very strongly'

Strong Pronoun, Lamas (Participant L L21)
(35) Y   un niño está # arrimando a   ella.
      and a boy is   # pushing   to her
      'And a boy is pushing it'

The lack of strong pronouns in bilingual Spanish coincides with their absence in the Quechua narratives from Ulcumayo and their very low frequency in Lamas (see Chapter 4). This could be an effect of the task, but it is noteworthy that it contrasts with the more frequent use of clitics.

To summarize, as in the case of the Quechua narratives, DPs were the most frequent type of direct object complement in the Spanish narratives of the three groups. Clitics were the second most frequent type. This shows that, despite the lack of overt clitics in Quechua, these are part of the bilingual Spanish grammar. However, the bilingual groups also showed some null objects with definite antecedents that point in the direction of interference in the feature specification of the head of the null D. Apparently, a distinction between overt clitic pronouns and null pronouns is developing in bilingual Spanish. This distinction will be further discussed in the next sub-section. Evidence of convergence in morphosyntactic features was also found in the neutralization of gender marking in clitics, as indicated by the strong preference shown in the narratives for the gender-neutral dative form *le*. CLLD structures were found in the bilinguals. This shows activation of the Spanish Cl feature specification and correlates with bilingual Quechua SVO word orders. A preference for VO over OV word orders among bilinguals also shows the activation of features that involve verb movement although some interference from Quechua was found in cases of OV word order. Finally, CP complements were less frequent among bilinguals, presumably indicating avoidance of CP configurations. No evidence of extended use of strong pronouns was found and this is consistent with similar findings for the same task in Quechua.

5.1.3 Distribution of direct object antecedents

In order to determine the similarities and differences between the different discourses strategies used to recover topics in the two languages, I analyzed the distribution of direct object antecedents in the same way they were analyzed for Quechua (see Chapter 4). I found that, for the three groups, the most frequent direct object antecedent is an overt DP (either a subject or an object DP), as it is in Quechua. Unlike in the Quechua data, clitics and clitic doubling structures were more frequent in the Spanish data as antecedents, and null pronouns were less frequent in the Spanish narratives than in the Quechua ones.

Table 7. Distribution of direct object antecedents in the Spanish narratives

Antecedent	San Juan		Lamas		Ulcumayo	
DP (Determiner Phrase)	287	(44.9%)	355	(49.5%)	345	(51.3%)
Clitic	94	(14.7%)	72	(10.0%)	58	(8.6%)
Clitic doubling (DP)	71	(11.1%)	53	(7.4%)	36	(5.4%)
Not in the text	112	(17.5%)	141	(19.7%)	117	(17.4%)
Null Pronoun	26	(4.1%)	31	(4.3%)	50	(7.4%)
Complex antecedent	29	(4.5%)	26	(3.6%)	25	(3.7%)
Not recognizable	5	(0.8%)	19	(2.6%)	24	(3.6%)
Clitic Left Dislocation	6	(0.9%)	7	(1.0%)	10	(1.5%)
Strong Pronoun/Demonstrative	5	(0.8%)	3	(0.4%)	3	(0.4%)
Clitic doubling (Pronoun/Strong pronoun/Demonstrative)	3	(0.5%)	4	(0.6%)	3	(0.4%)
CP (Complement Phrase)	1	(0.2%)	6	(0.8%)	0	(0.0%)
Duplicated clitic	0	(0.0%)	0	(0.0%)	1	(0.1%)
Total	639	(100%)	717	(100%)	672	(100%)

SJM, L, U $p < 0.000007$
L, U $p < 0.072295$

Overt DPs appeared more frequently as antecedents in the narratives of bilinguals than in the narratives of the monolingual children. Among bilinguals, they appeared slightly less frequently in the Spanish than in the Quechua narratives. In general, DPs were used in this task to introduce new topics. This use is illustrated by example (37) from a monolingual narrative:

San Juan de Miraflores (Participant SJ36)
(36) *INT: A   ver CHI # cuéntame.
             let's see CHI# tell me
             'Let's see CHI, tell me'

(37) *CHI: Un niño$_i$ está viendo   una caja$_j$.
            a boy$_i$ is   looking at a   box$_j$
            'A boy is looking at a box'

Sentence (37) is the beginning of discourse and in it the child uses two indefinite DPs *un niño* 'a boy' and *una caja* 'a box' to introduce two new topics in discourse.

Unlike in the Quechua narratives in which the second most frequent antecedents were null objects, in the Spanish narratives produced by bilinguals the second most frequent antecedent type were antecedents that are not present in the oral discourse but can be identified by looking at the pictures. This type of antecedent was more frequent in the narratives of the bilingual children in Lamas than in the other groups. Their frequency in Spanish is similar to that of the Lamas Quechua narratives (24%). In this case, the speakers were relying heavily on what is assumed to be knowledge shared by the interlocutor, particularly since the interviewers looked at the set of pictures together with the child participant while conducting the interview. An excerpt from a bilingual narrative from Lamas illustrates this type of antecedent:

Lamas (Participant L3)
(38) *CHI: Este hombre # está tocando   un cartoncito,
            this man   is touching a cardboard
            'This man is touching a little carboard'
(39) *CHI: habiendo su perro y   su sapo # y   su motelu.[10]
            having   his dog and his frog and his turtle
            'there being his dog and his frog and his turtle'
(40) *CHI: Este hombre está abriendo pro.
            this man   is   opening pro
            'This man is opening it'

In this example the null object refers to the box that the boy is opening in the picture (see Figure 2 in Appendix I). This discourse strategy, elicited by the story-telling task, might be indicative of a deictic function that is constantly at play in the selection of overt DPs, clitics and null pronouns for bilinguals and that is particularly preferred by the Lamas bilinguals.

---

10. The use of the gerund form *habiendo* 'there being' in this sentence is not acceptable in monolingual Standard varieties of Spanish.

Clitics and clitic doubling structures were more frequent as antecedents in the San Juan narratives than in the bilingual ones. Nevertheless, clitic-related structures did appear as antecedents in all groups indicating that they are a crucial component of the topic recovery strategies of bilinguals.

Null pronouns were fifth in frequency, more frequent in the bilingual narratives from Ulcumayo (7.4%) than in the narratives of the other two groups. Let us recall that the Ulcumayo group had the higher percentage of null object antecedents in the Quechua narratives (39.9%). Although in general, null object antecedents were less frequent in the Spanish narratives than in the Quechua ones (see Table 12 in Chapter 4). This low frequency could be attributed to the presence of clitics that can be used in Spanish to recover topics. Thus, despite the fact that null objects with definite antecedents are present in bilingual Spanish, presumably due to interference from Quechua, they compete with clitics for the discourse-level function of topic recovery.

Other antecedents such as complex antecedents, unrecognizable antecedents, clitic left dislocation structures, strong pronouns, demonstratives, clitic doubling structures with strong pronouns or demonstratives, CPs and duplicated clitics had very low frequencies of occurrence. It must be noted that unrecognizable antecedents were more frequent among bilinguals than among monolinguals.

To summarize, the type of discourse exemplified in the Spanish narratives of the bilinguals relied heavily on the use of overt DPs and on the use of antecedents not mentioned in the text. Clitic-related structures were more frequent than null object structures across the three groups confirming their constant activation in Spanish. No significant differences in the distribution of antecedents were found between the two bilingual groups but significant differences were found between these two groups and the "monolingual" group. This indicates that, although bilinguals did not use exactly the same discourse strategies in their two languages, as evidenced by the lower frequency of null objects in the Spanish narratives in comparison to the Quechua ones, the two bilingual groups share some common strategies that may serve as cues to how interference and convergence operate.

5.1.4 Distribution of direct object complements according to their antecedent

A more detailed analysis of the relationship between antecedents and direct object complements was carried out to determine if similarities in distribution in discourse play a role in reinforcing interference and convergence in direct object structures. In particular, I looked for the role that DPs, CLLD and clitic doubling structures have in (re)introducing topics in discourse and the role that clitics and null objects have in the recovery of topics across discourse in bilingual Spanish. Let us recall that in Quechua, only DPs (re)introduce topics in discourse and only null pronouns recover them. If overt DPs recover topics in Quechua and CLLD constructions have similar discourse functions in Spanish, then one expects that this common role in discourse will contribute to convergence in the possibility of allowing for CLLDs in bilingual Quechua[11] and to some extent for clitic-less fronted topics in bilingual Spanish, as shown in Table 6 and example (30). However, CLLD constructions in Spanish compete also with clitic doubling structures, which are more frequent than topicalizations in the oral production of the bilinguals in this study. A possible way out of this dilemma is to assign DPs, CLLDs and clitic doubling constructions different functions in the recovery of topics.

I also expected that the constant activation of the null D in Quechua as a topic would have some effect on the null pronouns in Spanish. Notice however, that the null D structure competes with clitic structures for the same function. Again, one possible way out of this dilemma for the bilingual grammar is to assign slightly different functions to the recovery of topics accomplished by null objects than by clitics. In this subsection, I will show evidence that some specialization of the discourse functions of these structures is taking place in the two bilingual groups.

Table 8 shows the distribution of DP structures according to their antecedents. No significant differences were found between the two bilingual groups but they do differ significantly from the distribution of the monolingual group in particular with respect to the use of clitics and the use of null objects in Ulcumayo.

In general, for DP complements the most frequent antecedent is a DP. I will focus on some differences found in the use of DPs as antecedents of other DPs between monolinguals and bilinguals. Three basic strategies for DP repetition were found in monolingual narratives:

---

11. I assume that no actual morphological realization of the clitic features takes place in Quechua. However, it is their constant activation in Spanish that results in interference and convergence in Quechua.

Table 8. DP Structures according to their antecedents

Antecedent	San Juan de Miraflores		Lamas		Ulcumayo	
DP (Determiner Phrase)	85	(39.35%)	112	(44.09%)	132	(49.44%)
Not in the text	77	(35.65%)	106	(41.73%)	89	(33.33%)
Complex antecedent	19	(8.80%)	14	(5.51%)	14	(5.24%)
Clitic doubling (DP)	16	(7.41%)	5	(1.97%)	7	(2.62%)
Clitic	14	(6.48%)	9	(3.54%)	7	(2.62%)
Null	1	(0.46%)	3	(1.18%)	15	(5.62%)
Other[a]	4	(1.85%)	5	(1.97%)	3	(1.12%)
Total	216 (100%)		254 (100%)		267 (100%)	

[a] Includes CLLD, unidentifiable, strong pronoun, clitic doubling with strong pronoun.
Chi test SJM, L, U $p < 0.00009$
Chi test L, U $p < 0.065$

a. The repetition of an indefinite DP as a definite DP:

   San Juan de Miraflores (Participant SJ29)

(41) *CHI: Y   # parece que le   regalaron una ran-ita   chiqu-ita.
                and # seems that Cl<small>DAT</small> gave him a   frog-<small>DIM</small> little-<small>DIM</small>
                'And (it) seems that (they) gave (him) a little frog'

(42) *INT: Uhum # y   después ¿qué pasó?
                uhum # and then   what happened
                'And then, what happened?'

(43) *CHI: Bajó   a la   ranita con todos sus animales.
                put down to the froggy with all   his animals
                '(He) put the froggy down with all his animals'

In this case, the indefinite DP *una ranita chiquita* 'a little frog' in (41) becomes *la ranita* in (43).

b. The dropping or addition of a noun modifier:

   San Juan de Miraflores (Participant SJ36)

(44) *CHI: Está mirando ⟨al⟩ [//] al   sapito   que está dentro de la   caja.
                is   looking   at   the toad-<small>DIM</small> that is   inside of the box
                '(He) is looking at the little toad that is inside the box'

(45) *INT: Ya, muy bien ¿aquí CHI?
                ok   very well   here CHI
                'Ok, very well. How about here CHI?'

(46) *CHI: Aquí el niño cuando ya   cargó   al sapito   lo
            here the boy when   already picked up the toad-DIM ClACC
            está bajando   al   piso.
            is   putting-down on the floor
            'Here once the boy has picked up the little toad, he is putting it
            on the floor'

In this example the relative clause *que está dentro de la caja* in (44) is dropped in (46).

c. The restitution of the DP as a topic

    San Juan de Miraflores (Participant SJ19)
(47) *CHI: Pasó   un momento ⟨y⟩   [/] y   el niño vió la   caja.
            went by a moment   and   and the boy saw the box
            'A moment went by and the boy say the box'
(48) *CHI: Como sabía que era   su cumpleaños,
            as   knew that was his birthday,
            'As (he) knew that it was his birthday'
(49) *CHI: la   abrió.
            Cl opened
            '(He) opened it'
(50) *CHI: Sabía que su tío   le   había regalado pro.
            knew that his uncle Cl-DAT had   given   pro
            '(He) knew that his uncle had given him (something)'
(51) *CHI: Entonces abrió   la   caja.
            then   opened the box
            'Then (he) opened the box'

The DP *la caja* 'the box' in (47) is recovered as a topic by the clitic *la* in (49), but after the null generic *pro* in (50), the DP *la caja* 'the box' restitutes the topic in (51).

In the bilingual narratives, strategy (a) was the most frequent one. The following example from a bilingual narrative from Lamas illustrates this:

    Lamas (Participant L7)
(52) *CHI: Ahí   veo un caja # un motelu, un niñito, un sapito,   un perro.
            there I see a box # a turtle   a boy   a little toad a dog
            'I see there a box, a turtle, a boy, a little toad, a dog'
(53) *INT: Uhum # y   ¿qué pasó   después?
            uhum # and what happened after
            'Uhum, and what happened next?'

(54) *CHI: Después está [/] está abriendo la   caja.
             after   is [/] is opening   the box
             'Then (he) is opening the box'

Strategy (b) was very infrequent because, in general, the bilingual children made less use of adjectival modifiers or relative clauses. Strategy (c) was frequent in the bilingual narratives and is illustrated by the following example from a bilingual narrative from Ulcumayo:

Ulcumayo (Participant U18)

(55) *CHI: Y el niño está (a)garrando la cajita.
             'And the boy is grabbing the box'

(56) *INT: Mhum

(57) *CHI: Y   la   tortuga mira pro.
             and the turtle   looks pro
             'and the turtle looks'

(58) *INT: Mhum#

(59) *CHI: Sí   mira pro.
             yes look pro
             'Yes, (he) looks (at him)'

(60) *INT: Y   después ¿qué pasó?
             and after   what happened?
             'And then, what happened?'

(61) *CHI: El sapo está triste
             'The toad is sad'

(62) *CHI: y la tortuga se ríe.
             'And the turtle laughs'

(63) *CHI: El perro está mirando la caja.
             'The dog is looking at the box'

Sentences (55)–(63) comprise a fragment of discourse that begins with *la cajita* 'the little box' as a direct object in (55). Sentences (60)–(62) show a change of topic in discourse. In order to recover *la cajita* as the topic the full DP *la caja* 'the box' is re-introduced in (63). In these cases, I considered that a DP had as its closest antecedent in discourse another DP. I would like to point out that strategies a and c involve the constant activation of definiteness features. As predicted by the Functional Convergence Hypothesis such activation correlates with the emergence of overt markers of definiteness values such as the indefinite determiner found in the Quechua narratives.

After DPs, the second most frequent type of antecedents is the one that is not expressed in the text. This indicates that DPs tend to be the first expression of a referent that is observable in the pictures (see example (40)). For both bilingual groups, this deictic use of the DP is more frequent in the Spanish narratives than in the Quechua narratives in which the second most frequent type of antecedents were null objects. Thus, in this task bilinguals exhibit a similar behavior to that of monolinguals with respect to the use of DPs to introduce a topic present in the context but not in the discourse.

The third most frequent category consisted of complex antecedents, that is, cases of DP coordination. Complex antecedents had a slightly higher frequency in the monolingual narratives than in the bilingual narratives. The following examples illustrate the case of a DP with complex antecedent:

San Juan de Miraflores (Participant SJ 35)

(64) *CHI: El niño ponió [al   sapo y   al   sap-ito]ᵢ en la
            the boy put   to the toad and the toad-DIM on the
            tortuguita.¹²
            turtle
            'The boy put the toad and the little toad on the turtle'

(65) *CHI: El sapo malvado botó   al   sap-itoᵢ.
            the toad mean   knocked over the toad-DIM
            'The mean toad knocked over the little toad'.

Cases of complex antecedents were rare in the Quechua narratives and no clear comparisons with them can be drawn.

Significant differences between the monolingual and the bilingual groups were found in clitic and clitic doubling structures as antecedents for DPs. These were more frequent in the monolingual data than in the bilingual data. In the monolingual data, clitics were antecedents to full DPs in fragments of discourse in which a new topic had been introduced. The full DP recovered the old topic. The following example illustrates this point:

San Juan de Miraflores (Participant SJ 35)

(66) Aquí ⟨la⟩   [/] el sapitoᵢ viene contento a la casa ⟨de⟩ [//]
     here ⟨the⟩ [/] the toad-DIMᵢ comes happy   to the house ⟨of⟩ [//]
     del   niño
     of the boy
     'Here the little toad comes to the boy's house (looking) happy'

---

12. The form 'ponió' is a regularization of the irregular past form 'puso'.

(67) y el perro está contento
      'and the dog is happy'
(68) y el niño le₁   está saludando.
      and the boy ClDAT₁ is greeting
      'and the boy is greeting him'
(69) La rana está feliz
      'The frog is happy'
(70) y la tortuga está feliz por ver al   sapito₁.
      and the turtle is happy for see to-the toad-DIM₁
      'and the turtle is happy to see the little toad'

In sentence (68) the clitic refers back to the DP *el sapito* 'the little toad' in (66) but when *la rana* 'the frog' (69) is introduced in discourse and changes the topic, a full DP is required in (70) to re-introduce *el sapito* 'the little toad' as a secondary topic.

Finally, null pronouns in subject and direct object positions had a higher frequency as DP antecedents in the bilingual narratives in Ulcumayo, which seem to be more affected by convergence with the Quechua functional features. Null pronouns in the narratives from Ulcumayo were antecedents to DPs in contexts similar to those in which clitics were DP antecedents in the monolingual narratives, namely, when a change of topic had occurred and the DP reintroduced the direct object as a discourse topic. The following example illustrates this:

       Ulcumayo (Participant U14)
(71) CHI: El   sapo₁ (e)stá agarrado ⟨al⟩   [/] al   # tortuga.
            the toad₁ is   grabbing ⟨to the⟩ [/] to the # turtle.
            'The toad is grabbing the turtle'

(72) INT: Mhum# Mhum# muy bien
            'Uhum, Uhum, very well'

(73)   ¿Qué está haciendo el niño?
            what is doing   the boy
            'What is the boy doing?'

(74) CHI: Pro₁ (es)tá mirado pro₁.
            pro₁ is   looked pro₁
            '(He) is looking at (it)'

(75) INT: ¡Ah₁ muy bien.
            'Ah! very well'

(76) CHI: Apuntando pro$_i$ con su mano.
pointing   pro$_i$ with his hand
'Pointing at (him) with his hand'

(77) INT: Después, ¿qué pasó?
after   what happened?
'What happened next?'

(78) CHI: El otro niño agarró su palo,
'The other boy grabbed his stick'

(79) Pro (es)tá apuntando ⟨al   sapo⟩ [/] al   sapo$_i$.
pro is   pointing   ⟨at the toad⟩ [/] at-the toad$_i$
'(He) is pointing at the toad'

In this fragment, the null pronouns in (74) and (76) refer back to the DP *el sapo* 'the toad' in (71) but once (78) introduces a new topic in object position, then the full DP is required to re-introduce the topic.

To summarize, DPs in the Spanish narratives were used to reintroduce a topic previously referred to by another DP, to introduce a topic that was part of the context but not of the oral discourse and they were less likely to refer back to clitic structures or null pronouns. They also activated definiteness features, a fact that supports convergence towards those features in bilingual Quechua. In general, when compared to the Quechua narratives (see Table 13 in Chapter 4), the Spanish narratives show a significant drop in null object antecedents for DPs, although such uses were more frequently found in the Ulcumayo Spanish data. This fact is relevant because the Ulcumayo group had a higher percentage of null objects antecedents for DPs than the Lamas group in the Quechua narratives. It supports the idea that a similarity in discourse strategy reinforces interference in the specification of the features of the null D.

CLLD structures are also used to reintroduce topics in Spanish discourse. The results for their type of antecedents show similarities in the three groups with respect to DP antecedents but not with respect to clitic and clitic doubling constructions, as shown in Table 9.

The three groups used CLLDs to reintroduce an antecedent previously referred to by a DP. In that respect bilinguals seem to be perfectly aware of the role that CLLD constructions have in reintroducing topics in discourse. Nevertheless, there were differences with respect to clitic and clitic doubling antecedents. Bilinguals in Ulcumayo showed a pattern in which CLLD structures had clitic antecedents in a context in which there was an intervening antecedent, as shown in:

Table 9. CLLD according to their antecedents

Antecedents	San Juan de Miraflores		Lamas		Ulcumayo	
DP (Determiner Phrase)	8	(50.00%)	27	(61.36%)	15	(42.86%)
Clitic	3	(18.75%)	4	(9.09%)	8	(22.86%)
Clitic doubling (DP)	2	(12.50%)	8	(18.18%)	1	(2.86%)
Other[a]	3	(18.75%)	5	(11.36%)	11	(31.43%)
Total	16	(100.00%)	44	(100.00%)	35	(100.00%)

[a] Includes CLLD, null pronouns, clitic doubling structures, strong/demonstrative pronouns, antecedents not in the text, complex antecedents, unidentifiable antecedents.
Chi-square test SJM, L, U $p<0.070$
Chi-square test L, U $p<0.008$

Ulcumayo (Participant U23)
(80) CHI: Aquí le$_i$ está pegando.
here Cl$_{DAT_i}$ is beating
'(He) is beating him here'
...
(81) CHI: Aquí el tortuga el niño xxx el sapo.
here the turtle the boy xxx the toad
'Here the turtle, the boy (incomprehensible fragment), the toad'
...
(82) CHI: El sapo está saltando acá
the toad is jumping here
'The toad is jumping here'
(83) CHI: y el niño está llorando.
'and the boy is crying'
(84) *INT: ¿Por qué?
'Why?'
(85) *CHI: Porque pro al &sa sap-ito$_i$ le$_i$ bota.
because pro to the toad-DIM$_i$ Cl$_i$ throws
'Because (he) throws the little toad away'

In sentence (80) the clitic refers to the little toad, sentences (81)–(83) introduce other topics and in (85) the little toad is recovered as a topic using a CLLD. This pattern was different from that found in the Lamas narratives. Bilinguals in Lamas had a higher frequency of clitic doubling antecedents than clitic antecedents for CLLD structures (Sanchez 2002), The following examples show this pattern:

Lamas (Participant L25)
(86) Ese wambrillo lo_i está metiendo en agua a su perr(o)_i.
 that boy Cl is putting in water to his dog
 'That boy is putting his dog in the water'

(87) A su perro_i lo_i está viendo.
 to his dog Cl-ACC is watching
 'He is watching his dog'

The CLLD in sentence (87) has a clitic doubling construction as its immediate antecedent in (86). This is an unexpected pattern because apparently no reintroduction of the topic is required. Let us recall that the option between a clitic and a clitic doubling antecedent does not exist in Quechua. In this particular case, the discourse strategies of the two bilingual groups diverge. Thus, CLLDs structures have DP antecedents and they serve the function of recovering topics in discourse, but they interact differently with clitic and clitic left dislocation constructions in the narratives of the two bilingual groups.

The third type of structure used in Spanish to recover a topic in discourse is the clitic doubling structure. The distribution of antecedents for these structures differs greatly for monolinguals and bilinguals as shown in Table 10:

Table 10. Clitic doubling structures according to their antecedents

Antecedent	San Juan de Miraflores		Lamas		Ulcumayo	
DP (Determiner Phrase)	88	(52.38%)	113	(62.09%)	62	(50.00%)
Clitic	33	(19.64%)	20	(10.99%)	11	(8.87%)
Clitic doubling (DP)	23	(13.69%)	14	(7.69%)	13	(10.48%)
Null	10	(5.95%)	11	(6.04%)	13	(10.48%)
Not in the text	3	(1.79%)	14	(7.69%)	7	(5.65%)
Complex antecedent	6	(3.57%)	8	(4.40%)	6	(4.84%)
Clitic doubling Strong Pronoun/Demonstrative	2	(1.19%)	2	(1.10%)	1	(0.81%)
Other[a]	3	(1.79%)	0	(0.00%)	11	(8.87%)
Total general	168	(100.00%)	182	(100%)	124	(100%)

[a] Includes CLLD, unidentifiable antecedents[13] and strong pronouns.
Chi test SJM, L, U $p<0.0001$
Chi test L, U $p<0.0032$

---

13. Unidentifiable antecedents were more frequent in the narratives from Ulcumayo.

The most frequent antecedents for clitic doubling structures across all groups are DPs (52%, 62% and 50%, respectively). This indicates that clitic doubling structures serve the function of re-introducing a topic in discourse for the three groups as illustrated by the following example from an Ulcumayo narrative. In this case the DP antecedent is originally in a subject position:

Ulcumayo (Participant U 14)
(88) *CHI: ⟨El & sa⟩ [<] [//] el   sapo$_i$ (es)tá mirando.
              the   the toad$_i$ is   looking
              'The toad is looking'

(89)   Y   tortuga le (e)stá   agarrando al   niño.
        and turtle   is grabbing to   the boy
        'and the turtle is grabbing the boy'

(90) *INT: Mhum#
             'mhm'

(91)   Y   después, ¿qué pasó?
        and after   what happened?
        'And then, what happened?'

(92) *CHI: El   tortuga le$_i$ (e)stá mirando al   sapo$_j$.
             the   turtle   ClDAT$_i$ is   looking at the toad$_j$
             'The turtle is looking at the toad'

The second most frequent clitic doubling antecedent for the monolingual and the Lamas groups are clitics but in much lower percentages, with the lowest rates in the Ulcumayo group. This is understandable given the overall lower frequency of clitics as antecedents in the bilingual narratives. For the Ulcumayo group in particular, clitic doubling structures were a more frequent antecedent than clitics and they compete with null pronouns, the fourth category in frequency for the other two groups. Clearly, the Ulcumayo data show that recovery of topics with clitic doubling constructions is preferred when the antecedent is a clitic doubling construction or a null pronoun. Referents that were not in the text but could be identified in the pictures were more frequent antecedents for the two bilingual groups than for the monolingual one indicating a tendency to refer to an element that is information shared by the interlocutor using a clitic doubling structure.

Finally, I would like to discuss gender mismatches between the antecedent and the clitic in clitic doubling structures. Monolinguals had an almost even distribution of the forms *le* and *lo* when the antecedent or the doubled DP was

Table 11. Clitic doubling structures with a DP antecedent according to antecedent's gender

Gender	Clitic doubling (DP)	San Juan de Miraflores	Lamas	Ulcumayo	Total
Masculine	Lo	31	17	1	49
	La	1	1	2	4
	Le	24	83	57	164
	Les	1	0	0	1
Feminine	Lo	11	1	0	12
	La	0	3	1	4
	Le	20	8	1	29

masculine. Bilinguals overwhelmingly favored the form *le*. In Lamas they did so even when the antecedent was feminine. This supports the idea that for bilingual speakers neutralization of gender overrides the case distinction in Spanish. Table 11 shows the distribution of clitic forms in clitic doubling structures according to the gender of the DP antecedent.

To summarize, the two bilingual groups seem to use similar strategies for the reintroduction of topics when DPs have other DPs as their antecedents. They all seem to make distinctions that pertain to definiteness features that are an indication of the constant activation of these features in Spanish for a particular discourse function. I have proposed that this activation can explain the emergence of an indefinite determiner in bilingual Quechua. All groups preferred DPs as antecedents for CLLD and clitic doubling constructions. The availability of CLLD constructions to reintroduce topics in discourse supports the notion that constant activation for a similar discourse function contributes to convergence towards ClP in Quechua. With respect to CLLD antecedents, the Ulcumayo group showed a preference for clitics over clitic doubling expressions while the Lamas group showed the opposite preference. Apparently, both groups are in the process of developing a different function for CLLD constructions in their topic-recovery functions. Finally, with respect to clitic doubling structures, all groups had a higher frequency of DP antecedents for them. The Ulcumayo group showed a slight preference for either clitic doubling or null pronouns over clitics as antecedents for clitic doubling structures. This is consistent with the pattern found in the Quechua narratives of this group in which they preferred DPs and null objects as DP antecedents to antecedents not present in the text.

Both bilingual groups preferred the clitic form *le* when the antecedent is masculine.

I propose that this indicates convergence in a form unmarked for gender. I would like to suggest that in this case, convergence has resulted in a selection of only those features of Spanish that are relevant to the topic/focus structure of the sentence and to verb movement such as definiteness.

I will turn now to the distribution of antecedents for clitic and null object structures. The distribution of antecedents for clitic structures in the narratives of the three groups did not differ significantly (see Table 12). For the three groups, the most frequent antecedent for a clitic is a DP followed by a clitic structure and a clitic doubling structure. Much less frequent were the cases in which a clitic had a null pronoun or a CLLD as its antecedent. This indicates that both monolinguals and bilinguals use clitic structures to spell out continuing topics in contexts that do not involve previous topic changes.

Table 12. Clitic structures according to their antecedents

Antecedent	San Juan de Miraflores		Lamas		Ulcumayo	
DP (Determiner Phrase)	100	(50.76%)	85	(47.22%)	109	(61.58%)
Clitic	38	(19.29%)	34	(18.89%)	24	(13.56%)
Clitic doubling (DP)	28	(14.21%)	24	(13.33%)	9	(5.08%)
Null	15	(7.61%)	14	(7.78%)	14	(7.91%)
Not identifiable	3	(1.52%)	10	(5.56%)	10	(5.65%)
CLLD	2	(1.02%)	5	(2.78%)	5	(2.82%)
Complex antecedent	4	(2.03%)	3	(1.67%)	1	(0.56%)
Not in the text	3	(1.52%)	2	(1.11%)	1	(0.56%)
Strong Pronoun	2	(1.02%)	1	(0.56%)	2	(1.13%)
Other[a]	2	(1.02%)	2	(1.11%)	2	(1.13%)
Total	197 (100.00%)		180 (100.00%)		177 (100.00%)	

[a] Includes CP, clitic doubling with strong pronouns/demonstrative.
Chi test SJM, L, U $p<0.158$
Chi test L, U $p<0.156$

In order to confirm the preference for clitics not marked for gender among bilinguals, I looked at the gender specification of their antecedents. Table 13 shows the distribution of clitic forms according to the gender specification of their DP antecedents. Although the three groups use *lo* and *le* as direct object clitics with a masculine DP as antecedent, the bilingual groups show a clear preference for the *le* form in these cases, whereas the monolingual group shows a clear preference for *lo*. In the two bilingual groups, there is at least one instance in which *la* appears with a masculine antecedent.[14] A different pattern emerges when the antecedent is feminine, the monolingual group has a similar distribution for *lo*, *la* and *le*, as if the use were random,[15] and the bilinguals, to the extent that they had clitics, used *le*.

With respect to the antecedents for null pronouns, the two bilingual groups exhibit very similar frequencies as shown in Table 14.

The most salient difference between monolinguals and bilinguals is that null pronouns for the two bilingual groups had antecedents that were identifiable

Table 13. Gender features of DP antecedents to clitic structures

Antecedent	Gender of DP antecedent	Clitic used	San Juan de Miraflores	Lamas	Ulcumayo	Total
DP	Masculine	Lo	38	18	12	68
		La	0	1	3	4
		Le	17	63	89	169
	Feminine	Lo	15	0	0	15
		La	11	2	0	13
		Le	19	2	4	25
	Undetermined	Lo	0	0	1	1
		Le	0	0	1	1

Table 14. Null pronoun structures according to antecedent

Antecedents	San Juan de Miraflores	Lamas	Ulcumayo
DP (Determiner Phrase)	5 (50.00%)	13 (35.14%)	21 (46.67%)
Not in the text	0 (0.00%)	9 (24.32%)	8 (17.78%)
Clitic	3 (30.00%)	4 (10.81%)	5 (11.11%)
Clitic doubling (DP)	1 (10.00%)	2 (5.41%)	4 (8.89%)
Null	0 (0.00%)	2 (5.41%)	6 (13.33%)
Other[a]	1 (10.00%)	7 (18.92%)	1 (2.22%)
Total	10 (100.00%)	37 (100.00%)	45 (100.00%)

[a] Includes 1 strong pronoun case in Lamas, 1 unidentifiable antecedent and 1 CP antecedent. Chi test L, U $p < 0.1298$

14. It is not clear whether this should be attributed to errors in performance.
15. These facts have been discussed in Camacho and Sanchez (2002).

in the pictures but not present in the oral text and there were no such instances in the monolingual data.[16]

This indicates that a deictic use of the null pronoun is possible in the bilingual Spanish grammar. The following excerpt from one of the narratives illustrates the case in which the direct object is null, although it refers to the box that is present in Figure 1 (see Appendix I) but is not mentioned in the oral text:

Lamas (Participant L29)
(93) *CHI: El   wamrillu (e)stá agarrando esa   latita.
            the boy   is   holding   that can-DIM
            'The boy is holding that little can'
(94) *CHI: Ese motelu   (e)stá viendo pro.
            this turtle is   looking pro
            'Turtle is looking (at the box)'

There were also null objects as antecedents showing that null pronouns in bilingual Spanish discourse behave as a continuing topic. Again, no such cases were found for the monolingual group. The following examples refer to Figure 10 (see Appendix I) and illustrate a case in which the child interviewed interprets the picture as if the boy were looking at some eggs (which are in fact stones), the child goes on to say that the toad is also looking at the eggs and the little toad and the turtle as well:

Ulcumayo (Participant U3)
(95) *CHI: un chibolo está ahí   con su palo viendo a unos huevos
            a boy   is there with his stick looking at some eggs
            'A boy is there, with a stick, looking at some eggs'
(96) *CHI: y   un sapo ahí está viendo pro$_i$ tam(b)ién.
            and a toad   is   looking pro$_i$ too
            'And a toad is looking (at the eggs) too.
(97) *CHI: y   un sapito chiquito (es)tá viendo pro$_i$ y   una tortuga.
            and a little toad   is   looking pro$_i$ and a   turtle
            'And a little toad is looking (at the eggs) too, and a turtle (is looking at them too).'

This pattern is consistent with the types of antecedents that null objects had in the bilingual Quechua narratives. As I suggest above, this common use of null

---

16. This confirms the data found in Sanchez (2002)

pronouns as deictic elements and continuing topics throughout discourse in bilingual Quechua and in bilingual Spanish reinforces convergence in the feature specification of the D that heads the null pronoun to cover definite antecedents in bilingual Spanish. With respect to the structures used for continuing topics, clitics and null pronouns, the Spanish narratives showed evidence that clitics had a similar distribution of antecedents for bilinguals and monolinguals. They also showed convergence in bilinguals towards the feature specifications of the clitic form *le* for masculine and feminine antecedents. In the case of null objects, there were clear differences in their use by bilinguals. The two bilingual groups showed patterns very similar to those of their Quechua narratives. This supports the idea that interference in functional features that is triggered by constant activation in discourse leads to convergence.

5.2 Picture-sentence matching task results in bilingual Spanish

In order to obtain data on the acceptability of different direct object structures in bilingual Spanish, a picture-sentence matching task was used to elicit the children's preferences for different direct object pronominal structures. The main goal of this task was to elicit the children's preferences for a particular direct object structure over another in a context in which the antecedent had been referred to in the question and could be seen in the picture. The questionnaire had 11 pictures followed by a question and a choice of two possible answers for the question containing different direct object structures (see example in Appendix II).

Five items involved choices between a null direct object and another direct object structure. These were a clitic, a clitic doubling structure with a strong pronoun, a strong pronoun and a DP. In the case of a null pronoun versus a clitic, two pronominal forms used for continuing topics competed. The expectation was that for bilinguals these structures would be equally acceptable while monolinguals would reject the null object. In the cases of a null versus a clitic doubling structure with a strong pronoun and the strong pronoun, a topic continuing structure was opposed to a focalizing structure. Note that the strong pronoun is a strongly marked structure in terms of its grammatical acceptability. This was supposed to favor the choice of null objects for all groups. Finally, in the case of a null pronoun versus a DP, a structure used for continuing topics was opposed to one that introduces topics. In this case, null objects were to be preferred by all groups.

Table 15. Null versus clitic (feminine, inanimate, −definite, +specific antecedent)

Group	Number of participants	Clitic	Null pronoun
San Juan de Miraflores	36	27 (75.0%)	9 (25.0%)
Lamas	30	13 (43.3%)	17 (56.7%)
Ulcumayo	28	15 (53.6%)	13 (46.4%)

The results were clear for null objects versus clitic structures, as shown in Table 15. Sharp differences between monolinguals and bilinguals were obtained when the three groups were given a choice between a null pronoun and a clitic. Most of the monolingual children preferred the clitic to the null pronoun. This is consistent with the fact that the monolingual children use clitics as continuing topics. The bilingual children, on the other hand, did not exhibit such a clear preference for either one of the forms. This is also consistent with the fact that bilinguals use null pronouns as continuing topics in discourse or as deictic elements and they also use clitics as continuing topics.

Table 16. Clitic doubling with strong pronouns versus null (feminine, animate, +definite, +specific antecedent)

Groups	Number of participants	Clitic doubling w/strong pronoun	Null pronoun	Other[17]
San Juan de Miraflores	36	27 (75.0%)	9 (25.0%)	0 (0.0%)
Lamas	30	16 (53.3%)	14 (46.7%)	0 (0.0%)
Ulcumayo	28	12 (42.9%)	14 (50.0%)	2 (7.1%)

In the choice between a null pronoun and a clitic doubling structure with a strong pronoun, the monolingual group behaved very differently from the two bilingual groups. This is shown in Table 16. They preferred the doubling structure to the null pronoun, that is, they preferred to use a focalizing structure for a referent present in the picture rather than a continuing topic structure. Perhaps, the other potential referents in the picture contributed to their preference for the focalizing structure. The majority of children rejected the null pronoun. The bilingual groups did not show a clear preference for either

---

17. There was no (c) option but in their replies some children altered either option (a) or (b). For those cases I have included this column.

form. Again, for the monolingual group, it was clearly the case that null objects cannot be used deictically and therefore they were forced to a focalized interpretation while the bilinguals had the possibility of interpreting the null object as a topic or selecting the focalized structure.

When the choice was between a null pronoun and a strong pronoun with a masculine antecedent, the monolingual population showed a clear preference for the strong pronoun, indicating that, although the strong pronoun is a very marked structure in Spanish (they were absent in the monolingual narratives), it was preferred to the null pronoun. The responses of the bilingual groups allowed for both forms. The bilinguals in Lamas preferred the null pronoun, but the bilingual population in Ulcumayo had a slight preference for the strong pronoun. In this case, 77.8% of the monolinguals did not prefer the null pronoun. These results are shown in Table 17.

Table 17. Null versus strong pronoun (masculine, inanimate, +definite, +specific antecedent)

Groups	Number of participants	Null pronoun	Strong pronoun	Other
San Juan de Miraflores	36	8 (22.2%)	28 (77.8%)	0 (0.0%)
Lamas	30	18 (60.0%)	12 (40.0%)	0 (0.0%)
Ulcumayo	28	11 (39.3%)	15 (53.6%)	2 (7.1%)

In the choice between a null pronoun that had a feminine, inanimate and indefinite antecedent and a definite, specific DP, the three groups showed a preference for the DP. This is shown in Table 18. Perhaps this preference can be attributed to the fact that the answer privileged the definiteness features in the DP. Nevertheless, 23% of the children in Lamas preferred the null pronoun to the DP. This indicates that despite the possible perception among the children that the question required the expression of definite features, some of the children in Lamas still used the null pronoun.

To summarize, monolingual children showed a clear pattern of rejection of the null pronoun when opposed to a structure used for continuing topics such as the clitic. They also preferred focalizing structures such as clitic doubling with a strong pronoun or strong pronouns to a null object. Bilingual children did not show a strong preference for null objects when opposed to clitics or focalizing structures and the two bilingual groups seemed to accept either choice. This is consistent with the findings in the narratives. Monolingual

Table 18. Null versus DP (feminine, inanimate, +definite, +specific antecedent)

Group	Number of participants	Null pronoun	DP	Other
San Juan de Miraflores	36	5 (13.9%)	31 (86.1%)	0 (0.0%)
Lamas	30	7 (23.3%)	23 (76.7%)	0 (0.0%)
Ulcumayo	28	4 (14.3%)	23 (82.1%)	1 (3.6%)

children showed lower frequencies of null objects than bilinguals and they did not use them for deictic purposes or as continuing topics while bilingual children did. This supports the notion that there is some interference in the feature specification of the null D that heads the null pronoun that is related to the frequent activation of null objects as continuing topics or as deictic elements. Such interference coexists in bilingual Spanish with the feature specification for Cl.

There were also three items that tested the preferences of the children when clitics were opposed to focalizing structures and to DPs that have the function of introducing or reintroducing topics. It was expected that in all cases the monolingual and bilingual groups would prefer the clitic as the expression of a continuing topic introduced by the question and identifiable in the picture. The results in these cases were less clear than in the case of null pronouns.

In the choice between a clitic and a strong pronoun, monolinguals preferred the clitic to the strong pronoun, as shown in Table 19. Bilinguals did not show a clear preference for either. In fact, three participants in Ulcumayo altered the choices.

Table 19. Clitic versus strong pronoun (feminine, animate, +definite, +specific antecedent)

Group	Number of participants	Clitic	Strong pronoun	Other
San Juan de Miraflores	36	23 (63.9%)	13 (36.1%)	0 (0.0%)
Lamas	30	16 (53.3%)	13 (43.3%)	1 (3.3%)
Ulcumayo	28	13 (46.4%)	12 (42.9%)	3 (10.7%)

With respect to the choice between a clitic structure and a clitic doubling structure with a strong pronoun, I found that neither the monolingual group nor the bilingual group in Lamas showed a clear preference. However, the bilingual group in Ulcumayo favored the clitic doubling structure. This result was not expected given that the clitic structure is associated with a topic and the doubling structure with a strong pronoun is associated with a focused element. Apparently, more of the Ulcumayo children had the perception that there was another potential referent in the picture (the turtle) and this led them to prefer the focalizing structure. The results are shown in the following table:

Table 20. Clitic versus clitic-doubling with strong pronoun (masculine, animate, +definite, +specific antecedent)

Group	Number of participants	Clitic	Clitic doubling with strong pronoun
San Juan de Miraflores	36	19 (52.8%)	17 (47.2%)
Lamas	30	17 (56.7%)	13 (43.3%)
Ulcumayo	28	10 (35.7%)	18 (64.3%)

Finally there was a choice between a clitic and a DP. The responses to this item grouped together the monolingual population in San Juan and the bilingual population in Ulcumayo. Both groups showed a preference for the DP over the clitic. The bilingual group in Lamas was divided. Preference for the full DP may be due to a tendency in the academic register to replicate the question in the answer. This is shown in Table 21.

Table 21. Clitic versus DP (masculine, animate, +definite, +specific antecedent)

Group	Number of participants	Clitic	DP	Other
San Juan de Miraflores	36	12 (33.3%)	24 (66.7%)	0 (0.0%)
Lamas	30	17 (56.7%)	13 (43.3%)	0 (0.0%)
Ulcumayo	28	7 (25.0%)	20 (71.4%)	1 (3.6%)

Unlike in the cases of null objects for which clear differences between the monolingual and the bilingual populations were found, in the case of clitics opposed to focalizing structures or DPs the results did not distinguish between monolinguals and bilinguals. Apparently, focalized interpretations of the answers were equally favored as the continuing topic interpretations.

Three questions were included to test the children's preferences for clitic doubling structures versus other structures. With respect to the choice between a clitic doubling with a DP and a DP, both the monolingual population and the bilingual population in Lamas showed a preference for the DP, which could be indicative of normativization standards, given that clitic doubling forms are not used in academic registers. Only the bilingual population in Ulcumayo preferred clitic doubling to the DP form. This is shown in Table 22.

Table 22. DP versus clitic doubling (DP) (masculine, animate, +definite, +specific)

Groups	Number of participants	DP	Clitic doubling(DP)
San Juan de Miraflores	36	22 (61.1%)	14 (38.9%)
Lamas	30	19 (63.3%)	11 (36.7%)
Ulcumayo	28	11 (39.3%)	17 (60.7%)

The choice between a clitic doubling structure with a strong pronoun and a strong pronoun also gave clear results for the monolingual group. They showed a strong preference for the clitic doubling structure over the non-grammatical strong pronoun. The contrast was less sharp for the bilingual populations although there was still a preference for the clitic doubling form over the strong pronoun, as shown in Table 23. This preference is consistent with the low frequency of strong pronouns found in the narratives and may be indicative of the fact that convergence towards the specification of clitics and null pronouns as continuing topics precludes the strong pronoun.

Table 23. Clitic doubling w/strong pronoun versus strong pronoun (masculine, animate, +definite, +specific antecedent)

Groups	Number of participants	Clitic doubling w/strong pronoun	Strong pronoun
San Juan de Miraflores	36	30 (83.3%)	6 (16.7%)
Lamas	30	18 (60.0%)	12 (40.0%)
Ulcumayo	28	18 (64.3%)	10 (35.7%)

When strong pronoun doubling was contrasted with a DP, the monolingual group preferred the DP. This was also true for the bilingual group in Lamas.

The bilingual group in Ulcumayo did not show a strong preference for either and the fact that they had instances of re-elaboration of the answer shows that they did not like either of the choices. This is shown in Table 24:

Table 24. Clitic doubling w/strong pronoun versus DP (feminine, animate, +definite, +specific antecedent)

Groups	Number of participants	Strong pronoun doubling	DP	Other
San Juan de Miraflores	36	13 (36.1%)	23 (63.9%)	0 (0.0%)
Lamas	30	11 (36.7%)	18 (60.0%)	1 (3.3%)
Ulcumayo	28	12 (42.9%)	12 (42.9%)	4 (14.3%)

These results show that monolinguals preferred clitic doubling structures only when contrasted with the strong pronouns. In the other cases the DPs were preferred. The Lamas group results were closer to those of the San Juan group. The Ulcumayo group differed in their preference for clitic doubling with DPs over DPs.

Finally, a question was included that opposed a DP and a strong pronoun. The three groups preferred the DP to the strong pronoun. Nevertheless, the bilingual group in Ulcumayo had a higher percentage of children that preferred the strong pronoun, as shown in Table 25.

Table 25. Strong pronoun versus DP (masculine, animate, +definite, +specific antecedent)

Groups	Number of participants	Strong pronoun	DP	Other
San Juan de Miraflores	36	5 (13.9%)	31 (86.1%)	0 (0.0%)
Lamas	30	5 (16.7%)	25 (83.3%)	0 (0.0%)
Ulcumayo	28	8 (28.6%)	17 (60.7%)	3 (10.7%)

To summarize, the results of this task showed a more coherent set of responses from the monolingual group than from the bilingual groups. Monolinguals tended to reject null pronouns whereas the two bilingual groups gave divided responses, indicating more flexibility or acceptance of null pronouns. Monolinguals also rejected strong pronouns (with the exception of one question) whereas bilinguals showed more acceptance of this form. Monolinguals also preferred clitics to strong pronouns and to null pronouns whereas the responses given by the bilingual groups were divided and did not show a strong preference for the clitics, the strong or the null pronouns. Thus, this task showed that for the monolingual children there were low levels of acceptance of null and strong pronouns as well as a higher frequency of acceptance for clitics. In general, the bilingual children did not exhibit strong preferences with the exception of a preference for DPs over null pronouns and for DPs over strong pronouns.

The results of the narratives presented in this chapter showed evidence of convergence in a feature specification of Cl unmarked for gender. They also showed evidence of convergence in the specification of the D that heads the null pronoun and its identification in discourse either as a continuing topic or as a deictic pronoun. There was also evidence of convergence towards the specification of ClP related to verb movement as shown by the frequency of SVO word order and by the activation of Cl in CLLD structures.

The picture–sentence matching task showed unclear results for the bilinguals. However, there were sharp differences between the monolingual group and the bilingual groups with respect to the choice between null pronouns and other structures. Monolinguals showed a tendency to prefer clitics, clitic doubling structures and even strong pronouns to null pronouns while bilinguals accepted null pronouns as well as other structures. This indicates that the grammar of the monolingual group diverges from that of the two bilingual groups with respect to the licensing of null pronouns. I have proposed that this difference must be attributed to the constant activation of a null D in Quechua in these bilingual participants.

CHAPTER 6

Conclusions

6.1 Summary of main results

The results of the study presented in this book show evidence of functional interference that leads to changes in the syntactic and morphosyntactic representations of bilinguals such as SVO word order, dropping of the accusative marker *-ta* and the emergence of an indefinite determiner in bilingual Quechua as well as the gender-neutral specification of clitics and the emergence of null objects as continuing topics in bilingual Spanish. They also show evidence in favor of the idea that functional convergence takes place when functional features not activated in one of the languages are constantly activated in the other. These were the cases of Cl and D features in Quechua-Spanish bilinguals. The role of activation is further supported by similar discourse functions for the two equivalent categories in both languages.

Based on Zubizarreta's (1998) and Ordoñez and Treviño's (1999) proposals for overt pre-verbal subjects in Spanish, I analyzed the pervasiveness of SVO word orders in bilingual Quechua as evidence in favor of convergence in the bilingual grammars of Quechua and Spanish in the projection and specification of ClP. The constant activation of clitics in the Spanish narratives support the view that Cl features are active in the minds of these bilinguals and force the projection of ClP in Quechua. The activation of Cl features results in overt verb movement to Cl. In bilingual Spanish, the use of the clitic form *le* unmarked for gender is evidence of functional convergence in the features that identify Cl.

Evidence of convergence in the functional features of D was also found in a slightly higher frequency of null objects in the Spanish bilingual narratives than in the narratives of the monolingual children. An analysis of the direct object antecedents in discourse showed similar patterns of null-object identification in discourse in bilingual Quechua and bilingual Spanish. These patterns further support convergence in identification strategies of null objects as continuing topics or as deictic pronouns.

The difference in the monolingual and the bilingual grammars with respect to null objects was confirmed by the results of the picture-sentence task. The monolingual children consistently preferred clitics to null objects and had of low acceptance of null pronouns in general. The two groups of bilingual children did not show strong preferences for null object or clitics. This is an indication that both types of direct objects are used as continuing topics.

In the Quechua narratives, evidence of functional convergence in the specification of D was found in the dropping of the accusative marker -*ta*, particularly in the Lamas data. In those data dropping coincides with the emergence of an indefinite determiner.

6.1.1 Differences and similarities between bilingual acquisition at the steady state and L1 acquisition

In comparing the bilingual Quechua data at the steady state and the L1 Quechua data, several differences emerge. While accusative case marking is robust in Quechua first language acquisition (Courtney 1998), the bilingual Quechua data, specifically the data from the Lamas group, show that accusative marking dropping is frequent and coincides with the emergence of an indefinite determiner. I did not find evidence of a high frequency of sentence-final subjects as was found in the L1 data. However SVO word orders were very frequent. Such SVO word orders are not frequent in monolingual L1 acquisition and I take this to indicate that they are the result of interference and convergence with the Spanish specification for ClP.

On the other hand, the comparison between the bilingual Spanish data and the L1 Spanish data show some similarities. The instability in the L1 specification of gender was also found in the bilingual data. Some deviant forms in clitic doubling structures regarding the features of the doubled element were also found. As in the L1 data, the bilingual Spanish data shows some flexibility in word orders. Finally, the early null objects found in the L1 acquisition data were also found in the bilingual data. I would like to propose that their pervasiveness is due to convergence in the discourse strategies used to identify them in bilingual Quechua and bilingual Spanish. The fact that null objects with definite antecedents are present at early stages in L1 acquisition might also contribute to their presence at the steady state in a language contact situation, facilitating convergence.

6.1.2 Similarities between bilingual and L2 acquisition

Previous studies on the L2 acquisition of Spanish direct objects by Quechua speakers have shown evidence of transfer in the feature specification of null objects from Quechua into Spanish. The bilingual Spanish data show that at the steady state there is convergence in the feature specification of D as well as in the strategies for its identification. With respect to canonical word order, while convergence in ClP was found, some instances of OV word orders coincide with data that are similar to cases of word order transfer from L1 Quechua into L2 Spanish. In the bilingual data such cases were low in frequency, but nonetheless indicate the projection of a Topic Phrase compatible with the analysis provided for Quechua. As in some of the L2 studies mentioned in Chapter 1, I found that strong pronouns do not become part of the steady state grammar of bilingual Spanish but interference in the feature specification of clitics does converge and becomes part of the steady state grammar.

6.2 Implications for bilingual acquisition theories

The main goal of the study presented in this book was to answer the question of how cross-linguistic influence is represented at the steady state in the mind of bilinguals who live in language contact situations, and to identify the linguistic mechanisms that allow for interference in some areas of the grammar. The results obtained support the Functional Interference Hypothesis, in particular in the bilingual Quechua grammar where interference in syntactic features has resulted in changes in word order at the clausal level and in the specification of D features. They also support the Functional Convergence Hypothesis, in particular with respect to the feature specification of two functional categories that are constantly activated in discourse in one of the languages, Cl and D. The constant activation of Cl and D in Spanish allows for their activation in the bilingual Quechua grammar, as evidenced in SVO word orders and the emergence of the indefinite determiner. The constant activation of null pronouns as deictic elements or as continuing topics in Quechua allows for the activation of the definiteness features that license a null D with definite antecedents in Spanish. The study also provides evidence for a common set of discourse strategies that guide convergence in the identification of null objects in the bilingual mind.

6.3 Future research

Several areas of research in functional interference and convergence at the clausal level that remain to be further analyzed are functional features not activated in Spanish but activated in Quechua such as verb movement triggered by focus features and evidentiality features associated with the complementizer category C. The Functional Interference Hypothesis would predict that interference in evidentiality features from Quechua into Spanish should result in syntactic changes and that constant activation of those features should result in convergence.[1]

At the DP-level, further exploration of the properties of the emerging overt determiners in bilingual Quechua is needed, in particular, with respect to the licensing of null nouns. Also, the difference in results obtained in Ulcumayo and Lamas Quechua with regard to accusative dropping requires further study.

Finally, while evidence in favor of interference and convergence in the feature specification of the D that heads null objects was found in this study, the differences between clitic doubling structures and CLLD structures and their relation to Focus/Topic structure of the sentence need to be further explored. The low frequency of clitic doubling structures with strong pronouns and DPs and of CLLD structures in the Spanish narratives did not allow for conclusive results with respect to their distribution in discourse. More experimental studies that are culturally appropriate need to be developed to probe into all of these areas of the bilingual grammar.

---

1. Escobar (1994b) discusses evidential uses of tense in Bilingual Andean Spanish that depart from the monolingual tense system.

Appendix

Appendix I

Figure 1.

Figure 2.

Figure 3.

Figure 5.

Appendix 163

Figure 6.

Figure 7.

Figure 10.

Figure 16.

Appendix II

Question 1

1. ¿El niño vio al perro?
   the boy saw to-the dog?
   'Did the boy see the dog?'

    a. El niño no lo vio
        the boy not Cl saw
        'The boy did not see (it)'

    b. El niño no vio al perro
        the boy not saw to-the dog
        'The boy did not see the dog'

Appendix III

Examples of suffixes in the Ulcumayo and San Martín varieties of Quechua
Ulcumayo
Noun and verb suffixes

a. Agash chaypi yakunayan
   'The frog is swimming/getting into the water/wants to get into the water.'

   Agash chay   - pi   yaku - na   - ya   - n
   frog demonstrative locative water rective emotive/durative 3sing.

b. Chaypitaqa rumimi kayan. Chaypita runa aywakuyan armawan.
   'Then (he) is with the rock. And then the man catches him with his weapon (stick).'

   Chaypita - qa   rumi - mi   ka - ya   - n   Chaypita runa aywa - ku   -
   then   topic   rock focus/val. be   durative 3sing   then   man catch reflexive
   ya   - n   arma   - wan
   durative 3sing   weapon instrumental

c. Chiwchi kichayun tapa.
   'The child open the lid (of the box).'

   Chiwchi kicha - yu   - n   tapa
   child   open   emotive 3sing   lid

d. Niño estabata agarrado cajunta.
   'The child is grabbing his box.'

   Niño estaba - ta   agarrado caju - n   - ta
   child is   confidential grabbing box 3sing acc

e. Huk runala shaykuya
   'A man is entering.'

   Huk runa - la   shayku - ya
   a   man   surprise   enter   durative

f. ¿Wambrachu kawaykan saputa?
   'The child is watching the frog?'

   Wambra - chu   kawa - yka   - n   sapu - ta
   child   interrogative watch   durative   3sing frog   acc

g. ¿Sapulaq agashta aytaykan?
   'The toad kicked the frog?'

   Sapu - Laq   agash - ta   ayta - yka   - n
   toad   interrogative frog   acc kick   durative   3sing

h. Huk niño rischarin huk saputa
   'A child woke the frog up.'

   Huk niño   rischa - ri   - n   huk sapu - ta
   a   child wake   responsive   3sing   a   frog   acc

i. Runaspis aywakuyanmi
    'They also say that the man is catching up.'

    Runa - s   - pis   aywa   - ku   - ya   - n   - mi
    man   reportative additive catch up reflexive durative 3sing focus/val.

j. Agashta wañuchin
    '(He) kills the frog.'

    Agash - ta   wañu - chi   - n
    frog   acc   kill   causative 3sing

k. Huk algo tortugata qawayan gepanta
    'A dog looks at the turtle from behind.'

    Huk algo tortuga - ta   qawa - ya   - n   gepa - nta
    a   dog turtle   acc. watch   durative 3sing behind prolative

Lamas, San Martín
Noun and verb suffixes

a. Sapunti suk apishka
    'With his frog someone is grabbing.'

    Sapu - nti   suk api - shka
    frog   inclusive one grab   progressive

b. Kawamun agashta
    'He looks at the frog.'

    Kawa - mu   - n   agash - ta
    watch   directional   3sing   frog   acc

c. Wambra waqapayan achkunta
    'The child makes his dog cry all the time.'

    Wambra waqa - paya   - n   achku - n   - ta
    child   cry   frequentative   3sing. dog   3sing   acc

d. Wambriyu waqaykan qawanakuptin
    'The child cries when he is seen.'

    Wambriyu waqa - yka   - n   qawa - na   - ku   - pti   - n
    child   cry   durative   3sing look   reciprocal   reflexive   subordinator   3sing

e. Suk wambriyu apinayaykan[1] saputa
    'A child wants to grab the frog.'

    Suk wambriyu api   - naya   - yka   - n   sapu - ta
    a   child   grabs   desiderative   durative   3sing   frog   acc

---

1. The suffix -*naya* (desiderative) may refer to an action that is presently taking place *apinayaykan* "is grabbing".

f. Sapo apinanpaq
   'In order to grab the frog.'

   Sapo api   - na   - n   - paq
   frog grab obligative   3sing   benefactive

g. Suk wambriyushi kichanirayaykan
   'They say that a child is opening.'

   Suk wambriyu - shi   kicha - ni   - raya   - yka   - n
   a   child   reportative open   auxiliary   frequentative   durative   3sing

Appendix IV

Table 1. Distribution of transitive verbs in Quechua narratives in Lamas

Token	Type	Verbs used[2]
1	28	*Abushay* 'to abuse', apitay 'to grab with the hand', *buscay* 'to look for', chukay 'to choke', chutay 'to pull', kinchay 'to fence, to round-up', maskay 'to look for', puchay 'to finish', pusay 'to carry', atiy 'to be able to', satikay 'to introduce', *sustonay* 'to frighten', tariy 'to find', tiyariy 'to sit', upyay 'to drink', *asustar* 'to frighten', levay 'to carry', *ver* 'to see', *abrikay* 'to open', *pasay* 'to visit', *lamer* 'to lick', kaniy 'to bite', altay 'to discuss', *enfaday* 'to upset', aytay 'to kick', sakiy 'to leave', aywikuy 'to get into', waytay 'to swim', away 'to knit'.
2	7	Aptay 'to catch', aysay 'to pull', *caminar* 'to walk', *cariñar* 'to caress', *cargay* 'to carry', manchay 'to frighten', yukay 'to lie'.
3	7	apay 'to bring', *botar* 'to throw away', *cargar* 'to carry', churay 'to put', *matar* 'to kill', *patear* 'to kick', wichkay 'to close'.
4	2	makanayay 'to want to hit', katiy 'to follow'.
5	2	*alsay* 'to raise', wañuchiy 'to kill'.
6	5	*Abrazay* 'to hug', apikuy 'to hold on', *montay* 'to ride', surkuy 'take away', wischuy 'to throw'.
8	1	Chapay 'to look for, to register'
11	2	Apariy 'to carry on the back', kichariy 'to open'.
12	1	Apinayay 'to want to carry'
14	1	*Agarrar* 'to grab'
14	1	Mukuy 'to bite, to chew'
19	1	Mikunayay 'to eat'
20	1	Markay 'to cradle'
24	1	*Apuntay* 'to point' (in the story to point witha a stick)
38	1	*Mirar* 'to look'
74	1	Apiy 'to grab'
156	1	Qaway 'to look'
512	63	

2. Verbs are listed in the infinitival form although they occurred mostly as conjugated verbs. Auxiliary verbs (in Quechua or Spanish) that co-occurred with them are not included. The lexical roots from Spanish are in italics.

Table 2. Distribution of verbs in Quechua narratives in Ulcumayo

Token	Type	Verbs used
1	51	*Abrasay* 'to hug', akachariy 'to burn', amunchuy 'to munch, to eat', antraray 'to fall on something', *asustay* 'to frighten', ataray 'to tie', *buscay* 'to look for', *casay* 'to hunt', chapiy 'to throw', charay 'to have', chiriyay 'to cool', churay 'to keep', *empujar* 'to push', qayay 'to call', 'qiqay 'to call', quy 'to give', hapiy 'to follow', hayay 'to call', hitay 'to throw', ichiyay 'to shine', kuchuy 'to cut', laptay 'to slap', *leer* 'to read', liguay 'to beat', *llenay* 'to fill', machariy 'to get drunk', *meti*kuy 'to put in', mitiy 'to put in', miyay 'to bite', panay 'to insult', perpikuyan 'see' (?), piñay 'to upset', puklay 'to play', quy 'to give', rabiay 'to be furious', rascar 'to scratch', qatiy 'to follow', 'riray 'to see'; rischariy 'to wake up', salvay 'to save', satiy 'to put in', *señala*y 'to point at', *tener* 'to have', *tocay* 'to touch', urayay'to lower', urquy 'to take out', *ver* 'to see', waqachiy 'to make cry', warkay 'to hang', yapiy 'to add'.
2	18	apiy 'to take', *apunta*yay 'to point at', *cariñar* 'to caress', quy 'to give', hishkan 'to frighten', ishkiy 'to fall' kaniyan 'to bite' kichay 'to open', machukashan 'to smash', *mieruy* 'to frighten', *patear* 'to kick', qawarayay 'to wash', qipimuy 'to carry', qitarayay 'to throw', tarayan 'to seat' rirg*ando* 'to see', *traer* 'to bring', wishgarayan 'to close'
3	8	Apay 'to bring', chutay 'to pull', gatiray 'to follow', *jalar* 'to pull', kay 'to have', magay 'to hit', kaniy 'to bite' tak*ar* 'to throw'.
4	6	*Aventar* 'to throw', marqay 'to cradle', *maskar* 'to bite', piñapayay 'to bother', risgay 'to look', *sacar* 'to take out'.
5	2	*Abrir* 'to open', gipiy 'to carry'.
6	1	*Takaray* 'to throw'
7	4	*Alsay* 'to raise', mikay'to eat', *pegar* 'to beat', taripakuy 'to reach'.
9	1	Wañuchiy 'to kill'
10	3	Aywiy 'to beat', *botar* 'to throw', *cargar* 'to carry'.
13	1	Margay 'to cradle'
14	1	Aptay 'to grab'
23	1	*Agarrar* 'to grab'
61	1	*Mirar* 'to look'
104	1	Chariy 'to catch'
257	1	Rirgay 'to see'
714	100	

Table 3. Distribution of transitive verbs in Spanish narratives in San Juan de Miraflores

Token	Type	San Juan de Miraflores
1	30	Acompañar 'accompany', alzar 'raise', asustar 'frighten', atrapar 'trap', cariñar 'caress', castigar 'punish', comer 'eat', cruzar 'cross', dar 'give', desobedecer 'disobey' destruir 'destroy' fastidiar 'upset', golpear 'hit', hacer 'make', lastimar 'hurt', levantar 'raise', odiar 'hate', pegar 'beat', pensar 'think', perseguir 'chase', prometer 'promise', rechazar 'reject', regresar 'to come/send back', sentar 'sit', soltar 'let go', subir 'raise', traer 'bring', unir 'join', usar 'use', volver a hacer 'redo'
2	14	Avisar 'tell', curar 'heal', echar 'throw', escuchar 'listen', jalar 'pull', leer 'read', maltratar 'mistreat', molestar 'upset', pasear 'stroll', preferir 'prefer', recoger 'pick up', regañar 'tell off', tocar 'touch', tramar 'plot'
3	5	Comprar 'buy', decir 'say', llamar 'call', saludar 'greet', sentir 'feel'
4	4	Acariciar 'caress', lamer 'lick', observar 'observe', saber 'know'
5	4	Bajar 'put down', seguir 'follow', tirar 'throw', tumbar 'knock over'
6	2	Poner 'to put', recibir 'to receive'
7	1	Resondrar 'nag'
8	1	Abrazar 'hug'
9	1	Patear 'kick'
10	1	Gritar 'yell'
11	1	Sacar 'take out'
12	1	Querer 'love'
13	1	Dejar 'leave'
14	2	Cargar 'carry', tener 'have'
15	2	Encontrar 'find', morder 'bite'
16	1	Empujar 'push'
17	1	Agarrar 'grab'
18	1	Abrir 'open'
19	1	Buscar 'look for'
20	1	Ver 'see'
21	1	Mirar 'look'
22	1	Botar 'throw'
717	68	

Table 4. Distribution of transitive verbs in Spanish narratives in Lamas

Token	Type	Lamas
1	25	Aborrecer 'hate', acomodar 'accomodate', acuchillar 'stab', arrimar 'push aside', avisar 'tell', bandear 'navigate a river', brincar 'jump', cerrar 'close', copiar 'copy', creer 'believe', cruzar 'cross', decir 'say', empujar 'push', esperar 'wait', fastidiar 'annoy', hombrear 'push with a shoulder', indicar 'signal', jalar 'pull', llamar 'call', parar 'stop', rasguñar 'scratch', salvar 'save', *siprar* 'peel', sumir 'suck in', tener 'have'.
2	11	Amargar 'upset', cuidar 'take care of', dejar 'leave', enterrar 'bury', espiar 'spy', golpear 'hit', hallar 'find', pisar 'step on', saber 'know', sentar 'sit', tirar 'throw'
3	5	Buscar 'look for', encontrar 'find', pegar 'beat', querer 'want', soltar 'let go'
4	3	Hacer 'make', poner 'put', tumbar 'knock over'
5	2	Cariñar 'caress', subir 'go up'
6	2	Asustar 'frighten', reñir 'tell off'
7	1	Meter 'put'
8	1	Llevar 'take'
9	1	Alzar 'raise'
10	2	Abrazar 'hug', patear 'kick'
11	2	Montar 'mount', sacar 'take out'
12	1	Comer 'eat'
16	2	Matar 'kill', tocar 'touch'
19	1	Apuntar 'point at''
25	2	Cargar 'carry', seguir 'follow'
27	2	Abrir 'open', *marka*r 'cradle'
28	1	Botar 'throw'
58	1	Morder 'bite'
87	1	Ver 'see'
95	1	Mirar 'look'
120	1	Agarrar 'grab'
639	78	Total types

Table 5. Distribution of transitive verbs in Spanish narratives in Ulcumayo

Token	Type	Ulcumayo
1	26	Abrazar 'hug', alcanzar 'reach', alegrar 'make happy', amar 'love', aplastar 'crash', arreglar 'fix', avisar 'tell', bajar 'lower', buscar 'look for', cerrar 'close', coger 'catch', cruzar 'cross', fastidiar 'upset', golpear 'hit', gritar 'yell', insultar 'insult', lamer 'lick', leer 'read', mojar 'wet', odiar 'hate', parecer 'look like', sentar 'sit', sentir 'feel', tapar 'cover', traer 'bring', voltear 'turn'
2	10	Dejar 'leave', destapar 'uncover', encontrar 'find', guardar 'keep', mandar 'send', morder 'bite', *qipichar* 'carry', rascar 'scratch', tirar 'throw', tocar 'touch'
3	4	Asustar 'frighten', empujar 'push', hacer 'make', patear 'kick'
4	5	Meter 'put in', molestar 'annoy', querer 'want', soltar 'let go', tener 'have'
5	2	*Markar* 'cradle', montar 'mount'
6	2	Llamar 'call', mascar 'chew'
7	1	Subir 'go up'
8	3	Cariñar 'caress', comer 'eat', matar 'kill'
9	3	Abrir 'open', apuntar 'point at', jalar 'pull'
10	1	Llevar 'take'
13	2	Cargar 'carry', seguir 'follow'
15	1	Ver 'see'
16	1	Sacar 'take out'
15	1	Pegar 'beat'
45	1	Botar 'throw'
138	1	Agarrar 'grab'
233	1	Mirar 'look'
672	66	

Bibliography

Abney, Stephen. 1986. "The English Noun Phrase in its Sentential Aspect." Unpublished Ph.D. Dissertation. MIT.
Albo, Xavier. 1974. *Los Mil Rostros del Quechua*. Lima, Peru: Instituto de Estudios Peruanos.
Appel, Rene and Pieter Muysken. 1987. *Language Contact and Bilingualism*. London: Edward Arnold.
Baek, Judy Yoo-Kyung. and Kenneth Wexler. 2002. "The Role of the Unique Checking Constraint in the Syntax and Acquisition of Korean Negation." MIT ms.
Baker, Mark. 1988. *Incorporation*. Chicago: University of Chicago Press.
Belazi, Hedi, Edward Rubin and Jacqueline Toribio. 1994. "Code switching and X-bar Theory: the Functional Head Constraint." *Linguistic Inquiry*. 25. 221–237.
Bernstein, Judy. 1994 "Topics in the Syntax of Nominal Structure Across Romance." Unpublished Ph.D. Dissertation CUNY.
Black, Nancy, Verena Bolli and Eusebio Ticsi. 1990. *Lecciones para el Aprendizaje del Quechua del Sureste de Pasco y el Norte de Junín*. Pasco, Peru: Dirección Departamental de Educación and Instituto Lingüístico de Verano.
Bonet, Eulalia. 1995. "Feature Structure of Romance Clitics." *Natural Language and Linguistic Theory*. 13. 607–647.
Borer, Hagit and Kenneth Wexler. 1987. "The Maturation of Syntax." *Parameter Setting*, ed. by T. Roeper and E. Williams. 123–187. Dordrecht: Reidel.
Camacho, Jose, Liliana Paredes and Liliana Sanchez. 1996. "Null Objects in Bilingual Andean Spanish." *Proceedings of the 21st Annual Boston University Conference on Language Development*, ed. by E. Hughes, M. Hughes & A. Greenhill. 1, 55–66. Sommerville, Massachusetts: Cascadilla Press.
Camacho, Jose. 1999. "From SOV to SVO: The Grammar of Interlanguage Word Order." *Second Language Research*. 15. 115–32.
Camacho, Jose and Liliana Sanchez. 2002. "Explaining Clitic Variation in Spanish" *Formal Approaches to Language Universals and Language Variation* ed. by M. Amberber and P. Collins. 21–40. Connecticut: Praeger.
Cerrón-Palomino, Rodolfo. 1976. "Enseñanza del Castellano: Deslindes y Perspectivas." *Reto del Multilingüismo en el Perú*, ed. by A. Escobar. 147–166. Lima, Peru: Instituto de Estudios Peruanos.
Cerrón-Palomino, Rodolfo. 1987. *Lingüística Quechua*. Cuzco, Peru: Bartolome de las Casas.
Cerrón-Palomino, Rodolfo. 1989. *Lengua y Sociedad en el Valle del Mantaro*. Lima, Peru: Instituto de Estudios Peruanos.
Chomsky, Noam. 1986a. *Knowledge of Language*. New York: Praeger.
Chomsky, Noam. 1986b. *Barriers*. Cambridge, Massachussets: MIT Press.

Chomsky, Noam 1993. "A Minimalist Program for Linguistic Theory." *The view from Building 20*. ed. by K. Hale and S.J. Keyser. 1–52. Cambridge, Massachusetts: MIT Press.
Chomsky, Noam. 1995. *The Minimalist Program*. Cambridge, Massachusetts: MIT Press
Chomsky, Noam. 1999. *Derivation by Phase*. MIT Working Papers in Linguistics 18. Cambridge, Massachusetts: MIT Press.
Cinque, Guglielmo. 1990. *Types of A' Dependencies*. Cambridge, Massachussets: MIT Press.
Clahsen, Harald, Sonja Eisenbeiss and Anne Vainikka. 1994. "The Seeds of Structure." *Language Acquisition Studies in Generative Grammar*, ed. by T. Hoekstra and B. Schwartz. 85–118. Amsterdam: John Benjamins.
Clahsen, Harald. 1996. *Generative Perspectives on Language Acquisition*. Amsterdam: John Benjamins.
Contreras, Heles. 1976. *A Theory of Word Order with Special Reference to Spanish*. Amsterdam: North-Holland Publishing Company.
Contreras, Heles. 1989. "On Spanish Empty N' and N*." *Studies in Romance Linguistics*, ed. by C. Kirschner and J. DeCesaris. 83–95. Amsterdam: John Benjamins.
Coombs, David, Heidi Coombs and Robert Weber. 1976. *Gramática Quechua: San Martín*. Lima, Peru: Instituto de Estudios Peruanos.
Courtney, Ellen. 1998. "Child Acquisition of Quechua Morphosyntax." University of Arizona. Unpublished Dissertation.
De Houwer, Anette. 1990. *The Acquisition of Two Languages from Birth: A Case Study*. Cambridge: Cambridge University Press.
Deprez, Vivian and Amy Pierce. 1993. "Negation and Functional Projections in Early Child Grammar." *Linguistic Inquiry*. 24. 47–85.
Deprez, Vivian and Amy Pierce. 1994. "Crosslinguistic Evidence for Functional Projections in Early Child Grammar." *Language Acquisition Studies in Generative Grammar*, ed. by T.Hoekstra and B. Schwartz. 57–84. Amsterdam: John Benjamins.
Deuchar, Margaret and Suzanne Quay. 2000. *Bilingual Acquisition. Theoretical Implications of a Case Study*. Oxford: Oxford University Press.
Diesing, Molly. 1992. *Indefinites*. Cambridge, Massachusetts: MIT Press.
Di Sciullo, Anne Marie, Pieter Muysken and Rajendra Singh. 1986. "Government and Code-Mixing." *Journal of Linguistics*. 22.1–24.
Dominguez, Rocio. 2000. "Quechua/Spanish Codeswitching within the Determiner Phrase." Unpublished M.A. Thesis. Carnegie Mellon University.
Eubank, Lynn. 1993/4. "On the Transfer of Parametric Values in L2 Development." *Language Acquisition*. 3. 183–208.
Escobar, Alberto. 1972. *El Reto del Multilingüismo en el Peru*. Lima, Peru: Instituto de Estudios Peruanos.
Escobar, Alberto. 1978. *Variaciones Sociolingüísticas del Castellano en el Peru*. Lima, Peru: Instituto de Estudios Peruanos.
Escobar, Anna Maria. 1990. *Los Bilingües y el Castellano en el Perú*. Lima, Peru: Instituto de Estudios Peruanos.
Escobar, Anna Maria. 1994a. "Andean Spanish and Bilingual Spanish: Linguistic Characteristics." *Language in the Andes*, ed. by P. Cole, G. Hermon and M. Martin. 51–73. Newark: University of Delaware.

Escobar, Anna Maria. 1994b. "Evidential uses in the Spanish of Quechua Speakers in Peru" *Journal of Southwestern Linguistics.* 13. 21–44.

Epstein, Samuel, Suzanne Flynn and Gita Martohardjiono. 1996. "Second Language Acquisition: Theoretical and Experimental Issues in Contemporary Research." *Behavioral and Brain Sciences* 19. 677–714

Everett, Daniel. 1996. *Why there are no Clitics.* Dallas: SIL and University of Texas at Arlington Publications.

Ezeizabarrena, María José. 1997. "Morfemas de Concordancia con el Sujeto y con los Objetos en el Castellano Infantil". *Contemporary Perspectives on the Acquisition of Spanish,* ed. by A. T. Perez-Leroux and W.Glass. 21–36.Sommerville Cascadilla Press.

Franco, Jon. 1993. "On object Agreement in Spanish." Unpublished Ph.D. Dissertation. University of Southern California.

Fujino, Hanako and Testusya Sano. 2000. "Some Notes on the Null Object Phenomenon in Child Spanish" *Proceedings of the 24th Annual Boston University Conference on Language Development, I-II,* ed by C. Howell, S. Fish and T. Keith-Lucas. 308–318. Somerville, Massachussets: Cascadilla Press.

Gal, Susan. 1979. *Language Shift. Social Determinants of Linguistic Shift in Bilingual Austria.* New York: Academic Press

Gallo, Pilar. 1994."¿Se Adquiere el Lenguaje sin Esfuerzo?" *La Adquisición de la Lengua Española,* ed. by S. López-Ornat, A. Fernández, P. Gallo and S. Mariscal. 59–65. Madrid: Siglo Veintiuno de España.

Genesee, Fred. 1989. "Early Bilingual Development: One Language or Two?" *Journal of Child Language.* 16. 161–179.

Grimshaw, Jane. 1990. *Argument Structure.* Cambridge, Massachusetts: MIT Press.

Grimshaw, Jane. 1994. "Minimal Projection and Clause Structure" *Head, Projections and Learnability,* ed. by B. Lust, M. Suñer and J. Whitman. 75–83. Mahwah, New Jersey: Lawrence Erlbaum Associates.

Hernanz, Maria Luisa and Jose Maria Brucart. 1987. *La Sintaxis.* Barcelona: Editorial Crítica.

Herschensohn, Julia. 2000. *The Second Time Around. Minimalism and Second Language Acquisition.* Amsterdam: John Benjamins.

Hyams, Nina. 1994. "V2 Null Arguments and COMP Projections." *Language Acquisition Studies in Generative Grammar,* ed. by T. Hoekstra and B. Schwartz, 21–55. Amsterdam: John Benjamins.

Hyams, Nina. 1996. "The Underspecification of Functional Categories in Early Grammar" *Generative Perspectives on Language Acquisition,* ed. by Harald Clahsen, 91–127. Amsterdam: John Benjamins.

Instituto Nacional de Estadística e Informática. *IX Censo de Población y IV de Vivienda 1993.* http://www.inei.gob.pe.

Jackendoff, Ray. 1977. *X′ Syntax: A Study of Phrase Structure.* Cambridge, Massachusetts: MIT Press.

Jaeggli, Osvaldo. 1986. "Three Issues in the Theory of Clitics: Case, Doubled NPs and Extraction." *Syntax and Semantics.* 19. 15–42.

Jake, Janice, Carol Myers-Scotton and Steven Gross. 2002. "Making a Minimalist Approach to Code-switching Work: Adding the Matrix Language." *Bilingualism: Language and Cognition.* 5. 69–91.

Kalt, Susan. 2001. "The Interpretation of Morpho-syntactic Features in a Second Language: a Study of Clitics in Southern Quechua-Spanish." Unpublished Ph.D. Dissertation. University of Southern California.

Kayne, Richard. 1994. *The Antisymmetry of Syntax.* Cambridge, Massachusetts: MIT Press

Koopman, Hilda. 1984. *The Syntax of Verbs.* Dordrecht: Foris.

Koopman, Hilda and Dominique Sportiche. 1988. "Subjects." ms. UCLA.

Landa, Alazne. 1995. "Conditions on Null Objects in Basque Spanish and their Relation to 'Leismo' and Clitic Doubling." Unpublished Ph.D. Dissertation. University of Southern California.

Lanza, Elizabeth. 1997. *Language Mixing in Infant Bilingualism: A Sociolinguistic Perspective.* Oxford: Clarendon Press.

Lebeaux, David. 2000. *Language Acquisition and the Form of Grammar.* Amsterdam: John Benjamins.

Lefebvre, Claire and Pieter Muysken. 1988. *Mixed Categories: Nominalizations In Quechua.* Dordrecht: Kluwer Academic Publishers

Leopold, Werner. 1939. *Speech Development of a Bilingual Child: A Linguist's Record, ii. Sound Learning in the First Two Years.* Evanston, Ill.: Northwestern University Press.

Leopold, Werner. 1949. *Speech Development of a Bilingual Child: A Linguist's Record, iii. Grammars and General Problems in the First Two Years.* Evanston, Ill.: Northwestern University Press.

Liceras, Juana and Lourdes Diaz. 1999. "Topic-drop versus Pro-drop: Null Subjects and Pronominal Subjects in the Spanish L2 of Chinese, French, German and Japanese Speakers." *Second Language Research* 15, 1. 1–40.

Liceras, Juana, Begona Soloaga and Alicia Carballo. 1992. "Los Conceptos de Tema y Rema: Problemas Sintácticos y Estílísticos de la Adquisición del Español." *Hispanic Linguistics.* 5:1–2. 43–88.

Longobardi, Giuseppe. 1994. "Reference and Proper Names: A Theory of N-Movement in Syntax and Logical Form." *Linguistic Inquiry.* 25. 609–65.

Lopez-Ornat, Susana. 1990. "La Formación de la Oración Simple: las Omisiones de Categorías Sintácticas (S/V/O) en la Adquisición del Español." *Estudios de Psicología* 41, 41–72.

Lopez-Ornat, Susana, A. Fernandez, P. Gallo and S. Mariscal. 1994. *La Adquisición de la Lengua Española* Madrid: Siglo Veintiuno de España.

Lozano, Anthony. 1975. "Syntactic Borrowing in Spanish from Quechua: the Noun Phrase." *Lingüística e Indigenismo Moderno de América.* Actas y Memorias del XXXIX Congreso Internacional de Americanistas, 5. Lima, Perú: Instituto de Estudios Peruanos. 297–305.

Luján, Marta and Liliana Minaya. 1984. "The Universal Consistency Hypothesis and the Prediction of Word Order Acquisition Stages in the Speech of Bilingual Children." *Language.* 60. 343–371

Luján, Marta. 1987. "Clitic Doubling in Andean Spanish and the Theory of Case Absorption." *Language and Language Use: Studies in Spanish,* ed. by T. Morgan, J. Lee and B. van Patten. 109–121. Washington: University Press of America.

Martin, Juan. 1996. "On the Syntactic Structure of Spanish Noun Phrases." Unpublished manuscript. University of Southern California.

Mayer, Mercer and Marianna Mayer. 1992. *One Frog Too Many.* New York: Dial Press

Meisel, Jürgen. 1986. "Word Order and Case-marking in Early Child Language. Evidence from Simultaneous Acquisition of Two First Languages: French and German." *Linguistics.* 123–183.

Meisel, Jürgen. 1989. "Early Differentiation of Languages in Bilingual Children." *Bilingualism across the Lifespan: Aspects of Acquisition, Maturity, and Loss*, ed. by K. Hylstam and L. Obler. 13–40. Cambridge: Cambridge University Press.

Myers, Sarah. 1973. *Language Shift Among Migrants to Lima.* Chicago, Illinois: University of Chicago.

Müller, Natascha. 1998. "Transfer in Bilingual First Language Acquisition." *Bilingualism: Language and Cognition* 1.151–171.

Müller, Natascha and Aafke Hulk. 2001. "Crosslinguistic Influence in Bilingual Language Acquisition: Italian and French as recipient languages." *Bilingualism and Cognition* 4. 1–21.

Muysken, Pieter. 1984. "The Spanish that Quechua Speakers Learn: L2 learning as Norm-Governed Behavior." *Second languages. A Cross-Linguistic Perspective.* 101–119. ed. by R. Andersen. Rowley, Massachusetts: Newbury House Publishers.

Muysken, Pieter. 2000. *Bilingual Speech: A Typology of Code-Mixing.* Cambridge: Cambridge University Press.

Nicoladis, Elena and Fred Genesee. 1997. "The Role of Parental Input and Language Dominance in Bilingual Children's Code-Mixing." *Proceedings of the 21st Annual Boston University Conference on Language Development*, ed. by E. Hughes, M. Hughes & A. Greenhill. 1, 422–432. Sommerville, Massachusetts: Cascadilla Press.

Ordoñez, Francisco. 1998. "Post-verbal Asymmetries in Spanish." *Natural Language and Linguistic Theory.* 16. 313–346.

Ordoñez, Francisco and Estela Treviño 1999. "Left Dislocated Subjects and the Pro-drop Parameter: A Case Study of Spanish." *Lingua.* 107. 39–68

O'Rourke, Erin. "Peak Alignment in Peru: Spanish in Contact with Quechua." Paper presented at the Linguistic Symposium on Romance Languages 33. Indiana University Bloomington. April 24–27.

Ouhalla, Jamal. 1991. *Functional Categories and Parametric Variation.* London: Routledge.

Paradis, Michel. 1985. "On the Representation of Two Languages in One Brain." *Language Sciences.* 7. 1–39.

Paradis, Michel. 1990 "Language Lateralization in Bilinguals: Enough Already!" *Brain & Language.* 39. 576–586.

Paradis, Johanne and Fred Genesee. 1996. "Syntactic Acquisition in Children. Autonomous or Independent?" *Studies on Second Language Acquisition*, 18.1–25.

Paradis, Johanne, Elena Nicoladis and Fred Genesee. 2000. "Early Emergence of Structural Constraints on Code-Mixing: Evidence from French-English Bilingual Children." *Bilingualism: Language & Cognition.* 3. 245–61.

Pardo, Marisabel, Jaime Doherty and Inocente Sangama. 2001. *Los Kechwa Lamistas y la Educación Bilingüe Intercultural.* Lamas, Peru: CEDISA.

Paredes, Liliana. 1997. "The Spanish Continuum in Peruvian Bilingual Speakers: A Study of Verbal Clitics" Unpublished Ph.D. Dissertation University of Southern California.

Park, Marinell and Elizabeth Wyss. 1995. *Lecciones para el Aprendizaje del Quechua de San Martín.* Documento de Trabajo 28. Yarinacocha, Peru: Instituto Lingüístico de Verano.

Parker, Gary (1963) "La Clasificación Genética de los Dialectos Quechuas." *Revista del Museo Nacional.* XXXII. 241–252.
Parker, Gary. 1976. *Gramática Quechua: Ancash-Huailas.* Lima, Peru: Instituto de Estudios Peruanos.
Pérez, Jorge. 1999. "The Psycholinguistic Basis of Andean Spanish Morphosyntax: the Role of Second Language Acquisition Principles in Language Contact." Unpublished Ph.D. Dissertation. Cornell University.
Pinker, Steven. 1984. *Language Learnability and Language Development.* Cambridge, Massachussetts: Harvard University Press.
Platzack, Christer. 1996. "The Initial Hypothesis of Syntax." *Generative Perspectives on Language Acquisition,* ed. by H. Clahsen. 369–414. Amsterdam: John Benjamins.
Poplack, Shana, David Sankoff and Christopher Miller. 1988. "The Social Correlates and Linguistic Processes of Lexical Borrowing and Assimilation." *Linguistics.* 26. 47–104.
Radford, Andrew. 1990. *Syntactic Theory and the Acquisition of English Syntax.* Oxford: Blackwell Publishers.
Raposo, Eduardo. 1998. "Definite/Zero Alternations in Portuguese: Towards a Unification of Topic Constructions." *Romance Linguistics: Theoretical Perspectives,* ed. by A. Schwegler, B. Tranel and M. Uribe-Etxebarria. 197–212. Amsterdam: John Benjamins.
Rivero, Maria Luisa. 1980. "On Left-Dislocation and Topicalization in Spanish." *Linguistic Inquiry* 9. 513–517.
Rizzi, Luiggi. 1993/4. "Some Notes on Linguistic Theory and Language Development: The Case of Root Infinitives." *Language Acquisition*.3. 371–393
Rizzi, Luiggi. 1994. "Early Null Subject and Root Null Subjects." *Language Acquisition Studies in Generative Grammar,* ed. by T. Hoekstra and B. Schwartz. 151–176. Amsterdam: John Benjamins.
Rizzi, Luiggi. 1997. "The Fine Structure of the Left Periphery". *Elements of Grammar,* ed. by Liliane Haegeman. 281–337. Dordrecht: Kluwer Academic Press.
Rozencvejg, V. Ju. 1976. *Linguistic Interference and Convergent Change.* The Hague: Mouton.
Romaine, Suzanne. 1995. *Bilingualism.* Oxford: Blackwell Publishers.
Ronjat, Jules. 1913. *Le Dévelopment du Langage Observe chez un Enfant Bilingue.* Paris: Librairie Ancienne H. Champion.
Sanchez, Liliana. 1996. "Syntactic Structures in Nominals: a Comparative Study of Southern Quechua and Spanish." USC Unpublished dissertation.
Sanchez, Liliana. 1998. "Why do Bilingual Spanish and Spanish in Contact varieties drop definite objects?" *Proceedings of GALA '97, Conference on Knowledge and Representation,* ed. by A. Sorace, C. Heycock, and R. Shillcock. 148–153. University of Edinburgh.
Sanchez, Liliana. 1999. "Null Objects in Contact varieties of Spanish" In *Formal Perspectives on Romance Linguistics,* ed. by J.-M Authier, L.Reed and B.Bullock. 227–242. Amsterdam: John Benjamins.
Sanchez, Liliana. 2001. "Discourse Topic Constraints on Left Dislocated Subjects and CLLD Structures." *Features and Interfaces,* ed. by K. Zagona, E. Mallen and J. Herschensohn. 255–266. Amsterdam: John Benjamins.
Sanchez, Liliana. 2002. "The Acquisition of Interpretable Phi-features in L1 and L2/Bilingual Speakers in Language Contact Situations." *The Acquisition of Spanish Morphosyntax,* ed. by J. Liceras and A. T. Perez-Leroux. 89–114. Dordrecht: Kluwer Academic.

Schaeffer, Jeannette. 2000. *The Acquisition of Direct Object Scrambling and Clitic Placement.* Amsterdam: John Benjamins.
Schwartz, Bonnie and Rex Sprouse. 1996. "L2 Cognitive States and the Full Transfer/Full Access Model." *Second Language Research.* 12. 40–72.
Sorace, Antonella. 2000. "Differential Effects of Attrition in the L1 syntax of Near Native Speakers." *Proceedings of the 24th Boston University Conference on Language Development,* ed. by C. Howell, S. Fish and T. Keith-Lucas. 719–725. Sommerville, Massachusetts: Cascadilla Press.
Sorace, Antonella. 2003. "Near-nativeness." *Handbook of Second Language Acquisition.* ed. by. M. Long and C. Doughty. 130–151. Oxford: Blackwell Publishers.
Sportiche, Dominique. 1992. "Clitic Constructions." UCLA ms.
Sportiche, Dominique. 1998. "Clitic Constructions." *Partitions and Atoms of Clause Structure.* London: Routledge. 244–307.
Suñer, Margarita. 1988. "The Role of Agreement in Clitic-Doubled Constructions." *Natural Language and Linguistic Theory.* 6. 391–433.
Suñer, Margarita. 1994. "V-movement and Wh-Phrases." *Natural Language and Linguistic Theory.* 12. 335–372.
Suñer, Margarita and María Yépez. 1988. "Null Definite Objects in Quiteño Spanish." *Linguistic Inquiry.* 19. 511–519.
Taeschner, Traute. 1983. *The Sun is Feminine: A Study on Language Acquisition in Bilingual Children.* Berlin: Springer-Verlag.
Thomason, Sarah and Terence Kaufman. 1988. *Language Contact, Creolization and Genetic Linguistics.* University of California Press.
Torero Alfredo. 1964. "Los Dialectos Quechuas." *Anales Científicos de la Universidad Agraria.* 2. 446–478.
Toribio, Jacqueline. 2001 "On the Emergence of Bilingual Code-switching Competence." *Bilingualism: Language and Cognition.* 4. 203–231.
Torrego, Esther. 1998. *The Dependencies of Objects.* Cambridge, Massachusetts: MIT Press.
Torrens, Vincent. and Kenneth Wexler. 1996. "Clitic Doubling in Early Spanish" *Proceedings of the 20th Annual Boston University Conference on Language Development, I-II.* ed. by A. Stringfellow, D. Cahana-Amitay, E. Hughes and A. Zukowski. 780–791. Somerville, Massachusetts: Cascadilla Press.
Travis, Lisa. 1984. "Parameters and Effects of Word Order Variation." Ph.D. Dissertation MIT.
Uriagereka, Juan. 1995. "Aspects of the Syntax of Clitic Placement in Western Romance." *Linguistic Inquiry.* 26. 79–124.
Van de Craats, Ineke, Norbert Corber and Roeland Van Hout. 2000. "Conservation of Grammatical Knowledge: on the Acquisition of Possessive Noun Phrases by Turkish and Moroccan Learners of Dutch." *Linguistics.* 38. 221–314.
Van de Kerke, Simon. 1996. *Affix Order and Interpretation in Bolivian Quechua.* Faculteit der Letteren. University of Amsterdam.
Volterra, Virginia and Traute Taeschner. 1978. "The Acquisition and Development of Language by Bilingual children." *Journal of Child Language.* 13. 595–597.
Vainnika, Anne and Martha, Young-Scholten. (1996). "Gradual Development of L2 Phrase Structure. *Second Language Research.* 12. 7–39.

Weinrich, Uriel. 1968. *Languages in Contact.* The Hague: Mouton. [First edition 1953] New York: Linguistic Circle of New York.

White, Lydia. 2001 "Crosslinguistic Influence Revisited: An L2 Perspective." *Bilingualism: Language & Cognition.* 4. 46–48.

Zagona, Karen. 2002. *The Syntax of Spanish.* Cambridge: Cambridge University Press.

Zubizarreta, Maria Luisa. 1998. *Prosody, Focus, and Word Order.* Cambridge, Massachusetts: MIT Press.

Zubizarreta, Maria Luisa. 1999."The Cl(itic) Projection in Questions". *Catalan Working Papers in Linguistics.* 7.253–277.

Zuñiga, Madeleine. 1987. "El Reto de la Educación Intercultural y Bilingüe en el Sur Andino del Perú." *Allpanchis.* 29/30. 331–346.

Index

A
Abney, Steven 107
Accusative 12, 22–24, 28, 29, 53–56, 95
Accusative dropping 86, 96, 98, 112, 156, 158
Activation 13, 15, 16, 42, 51, 53, 85, 86, 93, 96, 101, 103, 113, 128, 131, 132, 135, 142, 146, 155, 157, 158
Antecedents 15, 47, 50, 52, 60, 61, 82, 93, 104, 106, 107, 109–113, 115, 124, 128–133, 136–146, 155–157

B
Bare NPs 100
Borrowing 11, 14, 89

C
Camacho, Jose 7, 28, 50, 60–62, 116, 124, 144
Case 12, 22–24, 28, 30, 53–56, 64, 96–98, 115, 133, 156
Cerrón-Palomino, Rodolfo 31, 37, 59, 68, 69, 99
Chomsky, Noam 1, 2, 8, 17, 29, 30
Clitic 6, 7, 15, 26, 28, 41, 45, 47–53, 57–59, 62–63, 95, 115, 116, 119–124, 127–129, 131–134, 136–144, 146–153, 155, 156
Clitic doubling 44, 47–53, 57, 58, 60, 62, 95, 108, 110, 116, 118–120, 123, 124, 129, 131–133, 136, 138–144, 146–153, 156, 158
Clitic-left dislocation 40, 43, 44, 126
  see also CLLD 40, 41, 43, 44, 126–128, 132, 158

Code-mixing 3, 4, 11, 14, 15, 96, 113, 120
Courtney, Ellen 54–56, 97, 156

D
D-features 17
Dative 26, 54, 95, 120, 123, 128
Definiteness 26, 46, 52, 99–101, 105, 106, 110–112, 115, 135, 138, 142, 143, 148, 157
Demonstrative 37, 54, 85, 92, 93, 96, 98–100, 106, 109–111, 113, 116, 119, 127, 128, 129, 139, 140, 143
Determiners 6, 10, 14, 23, 24, 28, 53, 64, 99–101, 110, 112, 158
Direct object system 1, 15, 17, 22, 29, 37, 40, 53, 81
Discourse particles 20, 28, 90
Discourse strategy 113, 130, 138

E
Escobar, Alberto 7, 59, 60, 66, 121
Escobar, Anna Maria 7, 26, 60, 116, 121, 158
Everett, Daniel 26, 48
Evidentiality 20, 21, 30, 34, 40, 42, 51

F
First language acquisition 8, 54, 56–59, 64, 156
Focus 19, 20, 30, 34–37, 39, 40, 42–47, 49–52, 61, 83, 91, 143, 158
Focus Phrase 31, 36, 39, 45
Fronted object 39, 43, 105
Functional categories 1, 3, 4, 7–11, 14, 15, 52, 53, 64, 65, 85, 86, 115, 157

Functional Convergence Hypothesis 1, 15, 42, 51, 52, 84, 85, 101, 103, 112, 135, 157
Functional Interference Hypothesis 1, 13, 42, 52, 84–86, 91, 103, 157, 158

G
Gender 6, 13, 14, 26, 48, 52, 57–59, 63, 64, 115, 120, 122, 123, 128, 142–144, 153, 155, 156
Genesee, Fred 1–3, 10
Grimshaw, Jane 17, 31

H
Head-Parameter 17–19
Hulk, Aafke 3, 13

I
Indefinite determiner 86, 98–100, 135, 142, 155–157
IX National Census 71, 72

K
Kayne, Richard 19

L
La 26, 44, 49, 57–60, 62, 63, 94, 95, 121–123, 133, 134, 142, 144
Lamas district 71
Lamas Quechua 5, 6, 11, 12, 18–22, 25–27, 31, 33, 36–38, 68, 70, 71, 96, 98, 103, 130, 158
Language contact 1, 3–5, 8, 10–15, 48, 54, 65–68, 74, 81, 84, 88, 156, 157
Le 26, 51, 61, 90, 94–96, 120–124, 126, 128, 133, 134, 141–144, 146, 155
Lexical categories 9, 13, 14
Lo 26, 48, 59, 63, 95, 119–121, 123, 126, 127, 134, 141–144
Longobardi, Giuseppe 107

M
Maturational Approach 9
Media Lengua 3, 11–13
Meisel, Jürgen 1–3, 54

Minimalist Approach 1, 17
Müller, Natascha 3, 10, 13
Muysken, Pieter 3, 4, 11–13, 38, 39, 56, 61, 96, 127

N
Neutralization of gender 115, 128, 142
Nominative 30, 36
Null generic pro 134
Null object 6, 37, 38, 58, 60, 62, 65, 102, 109, 110, 115, 130, 131, 138, 143, 146, 148, 156
Null pronoun 48, 92, 106–109, 112, 129, 141, 143–149, 153
Null subject 6, 24, 104, 127

O
Object agreement 17, 26, 27, 26, 28, 34, 38, 52, 56, 59, 64, 106, 123
Objective case 23
Ordoñez, Francisco 36, 40, 41, 46, 155
OSV 31, 32, 39, 45, 46, 51, 52, 104, 105, 127
OV 61, 101, 104, 126–128, 157
OVS 31, 32, 39, 45, 51, 52, 104, 105, 127

P
Paradis, Johanne 1–3, 10, 13
Parker, Gary 38, 68, 90
Phi-features 17, 115, 116
Post-verbal subjects 45, 46
Pre-verbal subjects 41, 103, 155

R
Rizzi, Luiggi 8, 20, 31

S
Second language acquisition 9, 59, 64
Sorace, Antonella 15
SOV 6, 12, 18, 29, 31, 32, 36, 39, 42, 52, 59, 61, 102, 103, 105
Spec–Head 17, 30
Specificity 24, 26, 48, 57, 98, 101, 106, 110–112

Sportiche, Dominique 29, 41, 48
Story-telling task 82, 85, 115–117, 130
Strong Continuity Approach 8
Strong pronoun 49, 92, 93, 109, 110, 119, 128, 129, 133, 140, 143, 144, 146, 147, 148–152
SVO 6, 12, 15, 19, 37, 40–42, 51, 52, 56, 58, 59, 85, 86, 96, 101–103, 105, 112, 123, 126–128, 153, 155–157

T
-*ta* 6, 22–24, 85, 88, 91, 96, 97, 96–101, 105, 112, 155, 156
Thomason, Sarah 4
Topic 3, 19, 20, 30–33, 36, 37, 39, 40, 42–44, 46–53, 62, 82, 83, 86, 91, 105–108, 110, 112, 115, 123, 127, 131, 132, 134–143, 145–150, 153, 157, 158
Topic Phrase 31, 39, 44, 46, 127, 157
Toribio, Jacqueline 3, 11
Treviño, Estela 40, 41, 155

U
Ulcumayo district 69
Ulcumayo Quechua 12, 18–22, 25–27, 31, 33–38, 68, 91, 96, 103, 112
Universal Grammar 1, 2, 8

V
Van de Kerke, Simon 23, 54
Verb movement 19, 29, 30, 36, 39–42, 47, 51, 52, 65, 103, 105, 106, 112, 128, 143, 153, 155, 158
Verbal inflection 89, 90
VO 37, 40, 52, 101, 104, 126, 128
VP 17, 20, 23, 29, 30, 32–34, 37, 39–42, 44–47, 51, 52, 89, 95–97, 104, 105
VP-insertion 95, 96

W
Weak Continuity Approach 9
Weak pronouns 26

X
XP-movement 19, 20

Z
Zagona, Karen 31, 40, 43, 44
Zubizarreta, Maria Luisa 19, 30, 41, 43–47, 155

In the series LANGUAGE ACQUISITION AND LANGUAGE DISORDERS (LALD) the following titles have been published thus far or are scheduled for publication:

1. WHITE, Lydia: *Universal Grammar and Second Language Acquisition.* 1989.
2. HUEBNER, Thom and Charles A. FERGUSON (eds): *Cross Currents in Second Language Acquisition and Linguistic Theory.* 1991.
3. EUBANK, Lynn (ed.): *Point Counterpoint. Universal Grammar in the second language.* 1991.
4. ECKMAN, Fred R. (ed.): *Confluence. Linguistics, L2 acquisition and speech pathology.* 1993.
5. GASS, Susan and Larry SELINKER (eds): *Language Transfer in Language Learning.* Revised edition. 1992.
6. THOMAS, Margaret: *Knowledge of Reflexives in a Second Language.* 1993.
7. MEISEL, Jürgen M. (ed.): *Bilingual First Language Acquisition. French and German grammatical development.* 1994.
8. HOEKSTRA, Teun and Bonnie SCHWARTZ (eds): *Language Acquisition Studies in Generative Grammar.* 1994.
9. ADONE, Dany: *The Acquisition of Mauritian Creole.* 1994.
10. LAKSHMANAN, Usha: *Universal Grammar in Child Second Language Acquisition. Null subjects and morphological uniformity.* 1994.
11. YIP, Virginia: *Interlanguage and Learnability. From Chinese to English.* 1995.
12. JUFFS, Alan: *Learnability and the Lexicon. Theories and second language acquisition research.* 1996.
13. ALLEN, Shanley: *Aspects of Argument Structure Acquisition in Inuktitut.* 1996.
14. CLAHSEN, Harald (ed.): *Generative Perspectives on Language Acquisition. Empirical findings, theoretical considerations and crosslinguistic comparisons.* 1996.
15. BRINKMANN, Ursula: *The Locative Alternation in German. Its structure and acquisition.* 1997.
16. HANNAHS, S.J. and Martha YOUNG-SCHOLTEN (eds): *Focus on Phonological Acquisition.* 1997.
17. ARCHIBALD, John: *Second Language Phonology.* 1998.
18. KLEIN, Elaine C. and Gita MARTOHARDJONO (eds): *The Development of Second Language Grammars. A generative approach.* 1999.
19. BECK, Maria-Luise (ed.): *Morphology and its Interfaces in Second Language Knowledge.* 1998.
20. KANNO, Kazue (ed.): *The Acquisition of Japanese as a Second Language.* 1999.
21. HERSCHENSOHN, Julia: *The Second Time Around – Minimalism and L2 Acquisition.* 2000.
22. SCHAEFFER, Jeanette C.: *The Acquisition of Direct Object Scrambling and Clitic Placement. Syntax and pragmatics.* 2000.
23. WEISSENBORN, Jürgen and Barbara HÖHLE (eds.): *Approaches to Bootstrapping. Phonological, lexical, syntactic and neurophysiological aspects of early language acquisition. Volume 1.* 2001.
24. WEISSENBORN, Jürgen and Barbara HÖHLE (eds.): *Approaches to Bootstrapping. Phonological, lexical, syntactic and neurophysiological aspects of early language acquisition. Volume 2.* 2001.
25. CARROLL, Susanne E.: *Input and Evidence. The raw material of second language acquisition.* 2001.

26. SLABAKOVA, Roumyana: *Telicity in the Second Language.* 2001.
27. SALABERRY, M. Rafael and Yasuhiro SHIRAI (eds.): *The L2 Acquisition of Tense–Aspect Morphology.* 2002.
28. SHIMRON, Joseph (ed.): *Language Processing and Acquisition in Languages of Semitic, Root-Based, Morphology.* 2003.
29. FERNÁNDEZ, Eva M.: *Bilingual Sentence Processing. Relative clause attachment in English and Spanish.* 2003.
30. HOUT, Roeland van, Aafke C.J. HULK, Folkert KUIKEN and Richard J. TOWELL (eds.): *The Lexicon-syntax Interface in Second Language Acquisition.* 2003.
31. MARINIS, Theodoros: *The Acquisition of the DP in Modern Greek.* 2003.
32. PRÉVOST, Philippe and Johanne PARADIS (eds.): *The Acquisition of French in Different Contexts. Focus on functional categories.* n.y.p.
33. JOSEFSSON, Gunlög, Christer PLATZACK and Gisela HÅKANSSON (eds.): *The Acquisition of Swedish Grammar.* n.y.p.
34. OTA, Mitsuhiko: *The Development of Prosodic Structure in Early Words. Continuity, divergence and change.* 2003.
35. SÁNCHEZ, Liliana: *Quechua-Spanish Bilingualism. Interference and convergence in functional categories.* 2003.
36. BARTKE, Susanne and Julia SIEGMÜLLER (eds.): *Williams Syndrome across Languages.* n.y.p.